Issues in International Social Work

Issues in International Social Work

Global Challenges for a New Century

EDITED BY

M. C. HOKENSTAD

JAMES MIDGLEY

NASW PRESS

National Association of Social Workers

Washington, DC

Josephine A.V. Allen, PhD, ACSW, *President*

Josephine Nieves, MSW, PhD, *Executive Director*

Nancy Winchester, *Executive Editor*
Marcia D. Roman, *Production Editor*
Christine Cotting, UpperCase Publication Services, *Project Manager*
Patricia Borthwick, *Copyeditor*
Elizabeth Reynolds, *Proofreader*
Bernice Eisen, *Indexer*

First impression September 1997
Second impression June 1998

Library of Congress Cataloging-in-Publication Data

Issues in international social work : global challenges for a new century / edited by M.C. Hokenstad, Jr., James Midgley.
p. cm.
Includes bibliographical references and index.
ISBN 0-87101-280-4 (alk. paper)
1. Social service--International cooperation. I. Hokenstad, Merl C. II. Midgley, James.
HV40.I83 1997
361.2'6--dc21 97-36950
CIP

Printed in the United States of America

To my daughters Alene Anne, Laura Rae, and Marta Lynne,
with confidence that international living and education
have better prepared you for the 21st century

– M. C. HOKENSTAD

To Edna and Abdulhey Saloojee, two dear friends in London

– JAMES MIDGLEY

Matthew's USB HSC
Level 2 Room 310
Stony Brook
N.Y. 11794-8279
(631)444-3685

1 2 179240 03 Sale

0-00-010341-1 / 19
36663 IMPRINTED LAMINATED F 1.45
0-87101-280-4 / B
ISSUES IN INTERNATIONAL SOC 27.95 N

Subtotal	29.40
Total Tax	0.12
Total	29.52 *
Cash	30.00
*** Change Due	-0.48**

10:39 01/07/02
THANK YOU!!!

Matthew's UMB HSC
Level 2, Room 310
Stony Brook
NY 11794-8279
(631)444-3685

Subtotal
Total

*** Change Due

THANK YOU!!

Contents

Preface

This book is the result of feedback we received following the 1992 publication of *Profiles in International Social Work* (NASW Press). That volume provided an international perspective but focused on the role of social work in different countries. Although the work was well received and has been used extensively in social work education, many readers encouraged us to produce a sequel emphasizing global issues and their challenges for the social work profession.

Issues in International Social Work analyzes most of the key economic, political, and social issues currently affecting social work in an international context. Each chapter then explores the role of social work in addressing one of these issues both internationally and locally. We have chosen chapter authors who are experts in their subject areas and internationalists in their work and commitment. Their knowledge and dedication are reflected in their comprehensive analyses and recommendations for social work.

A new millennium approaches and the global dimension of the issues and interventions addressed becomes increasingly important. In this book we look to the future! We consider the growing significance of the international context in understanding social problems. We argue that the local role of social work will be more and more affected by the international environment. Thus, we hope that the book will challenge social workers around the globe to think and act accordingly.

We appreciate the support and hard work of a number of people whose behind-the-scenes efforts have contributed to the publication of this book. Linda Beebe, former executive editor of the NASW Press, was supportive during the early stages of the project. The present executive editor, Nancy Winchester, and her associate Chanté Lampton have been very helpful during the processing of the manuscript. At Case Western Reserve University, Theresa Wilson, Deborah Horne, and Emily Vosburg had major responsibilities for both international communication and manuscript preparation. Thanks also to Michelle Livermore at Louisiana State University for her helpful comments and advice.

M. C. HOKENSTAD
Case Western Reserve University
Cleveland, Ohio

JAMES MIDGLEY
University of California
Berkeley

1

Realities of Global Interdependence

Challenges for Social Work in a New Century

M. C. HOKENSTAD AND JAMES MIDGLEY

As we move toward the new millennium, massive change is taking place around the globe. This change provides opportunities as well as challenges for social work's role and functions both nationally and internationally. The end of the 20th century is a time when new realities of global interdependence demand an increased emphasis on the international dimension of social work and human services.

The end of the 20th century marks the end of an era of ideological conflict that divided the world into opposing camps. The Cold War ended with the triumph of democracy over totalitarianism in much of the world and has ushered in a new era that offers increased opportunity for interaction and collaboration across national boundaries. Increasing political and economic interdependence have contributed to an environment conducive to increased international contacts and collaboration among social workers and social work educators. In fact, there has been more international exchange among social workers in the 1990s than at any time since the first decade after World War II.

At the same time, social work remains a profession with a largely local orientation. Most social workers function within the context of a locally based service delivery structure. Their work, whether directly with individuals and families or at a community level, is locality focused. Although much of social work is heavily influenced by its national environment, including the funding and focus of social welfare policies and programs, at first glance social work practice does not appear to be immediately or directly influenced by global trends and issues.

However, it is increasingly difficult to function effectively at any level of professional social work without an understanding of the global environment. Forces beyond national economics and politics have a direct impact on local well-being as the economy becomes increasingly transnationalized and the global actors such as the World Bank and International Monetary Fund increasingly influence social policy within countries (Instituto del Tercer Mundo, 1997). Jobs, pension programs, and the type and amount of social services available in local communities are directly affected by such international developments. Moynihan (1993) argued that the continuing growth of the global economy may be driving the world beyond an order based on the nation state—at least in terms of influence on individual lives.

Social work with individuals at the local level also is increasingly influenced by problems of global scope. Chief among them is the growing tribalization of world politics. With the end of the Cold War and the decline of ideology as the major source of international conflict, ethnicity and religion have more and more become sources, not only of group identity but also of group conflict. Throughout the world, whether in Bosnia, Rwanda, or the Middle East, ethnicity and geography are creating an increasing number of conflicts and a rapidly growing number of refugees. By the middle 1990s there were, worldwide, 20 million refugees outside their own countries and 20 million more uprooted in their own countries (United Nations [UN], 1994). This is the largest worldwide diaspora of people in the history of the world. As a result, more social workers around the world are working with refugees from either their own or other countries.

Increasing ethnic diversification of societies is evident throughout the world. Although this is not a new development in some nations, it is a growing trend in many countries. North America has historically been a nation of immigrants, but now non-European immigration is changing the face of the continent and its countries. During the coming decade, members of groups of color will become a majority in some states of the United States. Migration from south to north in Europe and from Asia to Oceania is increasing the heterogeneity of historically homogeneous societies. Economic migrants along with political refugees produce cultural diversity that directly influences social work at all levels of practice. Social work in culturally diverse societies requires an understanding of the cultural roots of the different ethnic groups. The international roots of culture have current as well as historical significance for social work (Chatterjee & Hokenstad, 1997).

Growing poverty within nations and economic inequalities between them are a related global reality that affects social work. The decades of the 1980s and 1990s have witnessed a growing income gap, not simply because rich people are growing richer, but also because poor people are becoming poorer. Income inequality within industrial societies is evidenced by the growing earnings gap between skilled and educated members of the work force on one hand and underskilled and less educated employees on the other. Worldwide markets have been a major contributor to the growing inequality, producing what Frank and Cook (1995) called the "winner-take-all society."

Many developing countries, especially those in Africa and South Asia, have been particularly hard hit by this increasing disparity of wealth. There is a great gap in the quality of life among human beings around the world, and that gap is widening. In 19 countries, per capita income is lower than it was in 1960, and as many as 1.6 billion people are worse off than they were 15 years ago. One billion, three hundred million people in the developing world live below the poverty level, and of these 1 billion have no access to basic services such as safe water and primary health care. Eight hundred million do not have enough food, and 500 million are chronically malnourished (UN Development Programme, 1996). The magnitude of the problem is global and thus has an impact on social work roles and responsibilities throughout the world.

These are key global flash points that challenge social work today and will continue to do so in the next century. Additional challenges of similar scope and comparable importance are human rights violations, AIDS and other epidemics, and the deterioration of the physical environment. All are global in scope and must be addressed internationally as well as locally. At the dawning of the new millennium it is no longer enough to think globally and act locally. Global problems often require global interventions.

SOCIAL WORK RESPONSE

Social work is one of many players in the response to these realities of global interdependence. The scope of global poverty and the intensity of ethnic conflict require first political and economic responses by nations and international organizations. Global challenges require action on many levels by many actors. Nevertheless, these are problems that are directly related to social work commitment and expertise. Social workers at the local level are directly involved with the implications of international realities by working with refugees or helping displaced workers. At the national level in many countries, the profession is active in promoting economic and social justice policy. Internationally, social work organizations are increasingly active in combating human rights violations. Thus, it is essential for social workers to have an international perspective and understanding to be effective practitioners in today's world.

Although social work clearly has an important role to play in addressing global challenges, it has major obstacles to overcome to become a more effective player. Lack of status and resources affects social work in most countries and limits the profession's capacity to respond to pressing human needs. Throughout the world social workers are involved in the struggle for social justice, but they often act in the face of political oppression and promote human rights at considerable personal risk. Also, government policies and services delivery structures often limit rather than enhance social work roles. All these factors impede the profession's ability to respond effectively to pervasive problems locally, nationally, and certainly internationally (Hokenstad, Khinduka, & Midgley, 1992).

Social work remains a creature of its own destiny, however. Professional status is partly determined by the level of education provided for social workers. Political influence is enhanced by expertise and effective organization, and social work's impact is strongly influenced by the profession's own definition of professional priorities and practice preferences. Social work as a profession and social workers as professional practitioners have often been creative and innovative in responding to new problem-solving challenges. Midgley (1997) observed that this responsiveness to emerging issues has included an ability to engage in activities that diverge from the mainstream tasks of social work practice. The recent response to a problem of global scope such as the HIV and AIDS pandemic indicates a potential for social workers to become more relevant participants at the international level.

How then does the social work profession put itself in a position to effectively respond to realities of global interdependence? How do social workers become better prepared to be effective players on the global playing field? Answering these questions should receive high priority as social work charts its course for the new century. Discussion and debate about some of the specifics are necessary, and resource limitations must be recognized and addressed, but some answers are apparent. They involve action to strengthen the international dimension of social work.

One priority is strengthening the profession's international institutional framework. Several international organizations provide an identity for social work. Those most closely identified with the profession are the International Federation of Social Workers (IFSW) and the International Association of Schools of Social Work (IASSW). Both have active programs and involve social workers from around the world. IFSW has been particularly active in promoting human rights and protesting human rights violations, and IASSW has provided information and support that has internationalized educational programs and better prepared social work educators for international teaching. Both are active and productive but fragile organizations. Their base of financial support is limited, and their programs lack wide exposure among social workers around the world. With the exception of biennial congresses, few social workers are in contact with the programs of IFSW and IASSW.

Other international organizations such as the International Council on Social Welfare (ICSW) and the Inter-University Consortium on International Social Development (IUCISD) also have close ties with social work. These bodies function in the broad arena of social welfare and social development, but much of the leadership comes form the social work profession, and most of their programs are directly related to social work's international role. They, too, are fragile organizations and little known to most social workers.

All of these international organizations, along with others in specialized fields such as child welfare, aging, and mental health, provide vehicles for international social work involvement and action. As of now insufficient involvement as much as inadequate resources limits these organizations on the international scene. They serve a useful educational function and are sometimes effective in a gadfly role, but they need increased involvement and support from social work's national organizations as well as from rank and file social workers to become more of a force on the global scene. A strong institutional framework is requisite for an effective social work presence.

More social work involvement in the United Nations and international nongovernment organizations (NGOs) is needed. Social workers have provided some leadership in the UN Centre for Social Development and Humanitarian Affairs and in agencies such as the UN Children's Fund (UNICEF), the High Commissioner for Refugees (UNHCR), and the World Health Organisation (WHO), but this involvement has been limited to a small number of individuals. IASSW and IFSW are represented on a number of the NGO committees that are consultative to the UN Economic and Social Council (ECOSOC) and various UN agencies and thus create some institutional linkages. Currently, however, the organized social work presence at the UN is minimal and must be both expanded and better coordinated.

A few international NGOs such as International Social Service, have a strong social work presence, but most do not. International relief and social development agencies such as Cooperative for American Relief

Everywhere (CARE) and Oxfam have little social work involvement in spite of having many programs directly related to social work functions. Healy (1995) examined these international social welfare organizations and the limited involvement of American social workers in their programs and concluded that "In general, U.S. social work, the dominant profession in domestic social welfare, has remained uninvolved in international social development agencies, untouched by the development education movement, and uninterested in social welfare policy with international implications" (p. 1509). Clearly the organized profession and social workers individually must take a more active interest and role in the UN and international NGOs if social work is to effectively respond to realities of global interdependence.

If social workers are to become not only more involved but also more effectively involved in international organizations and global issues, the international dimension of social work education also must be strengthened. Educational programs for social workers around the world give only limited attention to social issues that extend beyond national boundaries. Most students have little if any exposure to international roles for social workers. The social work curriculum is crowded, and there is a perception among educators that international content is not directly relevant to the practice of most social workers. Although there is some international content in the curricula of a sizable number of schools of social work most of it is focused on cross-national policy and program comparisons rather than global issues and practice roles.

International concern and content receive only limited attention in programs of social work education in the United States. Individual courses are offered in many curricula, but international learning is most often an individual rather than an institutional activity, primarily as a result of student and faculty exchanges. These exchanges have been unbalanced, with the greatest flow of students into the United States and the flow of educators from the United States to other countries for teaching, research, and program consultation. There has been an effort toward a more balanced two-way exchange in recent years, but the overall pattern raises issues of reciprocity in faculty interaction and appropriateness in foreign student education. The exchanges can provide information and insights about the practice of social work in other nations, but not necessarily in international social work (Hokenstad & Kendall, 1995).

International exchange offers one potentially important way to energize social work's response to global realities. Exchange programs can provide experiential learning and expand the community of social workers within an international commitment. The Council of International Programs for Social Workers and Youth Workers (CIP) has successfully provided thousands of social workers with cross-national experiences and understanding for 40 years. Professional practitioners as well as students and faculty benefit from programs of exchange.

However, exchange should be extended from the individual to the institutional level if it is to have a full impact. Long-term bilateral interaction between agencies or educational programs in different countries can result in movement from exchange to collaboration. Program collaboration can be built on reciprocity, with both partners contributing to and gaining from the collaboration. It also encourages networking to involve a substantial number of individuals and possibly other programs in the exchange over a period of time. Finally, it can lead to institutionalization of exchange and have a permanent effect on both collaborating programs and their institutional environment.

Bilateral program affiliations in a cross-national context exist but are not common in social work education, and they are quite rare among social services agencies. Those that develop into a long-term collaboration are rarer still. An increase in the number and duration of such institutionalized exchange programs would provide expanded opportunity for social workers to become internationally educated. At the same time, it would strengthen the institutional infrastructure for social work's global role.

The major international challenge facing social work must be addressed in several ways. Education and exchange are both needed. A more fully developed and expanded international dimension to the social work curriculum, coupled with overseas field experiences, will provide better knowledge and skills for globally oriented social workers. Increased opportunities for exchange experiences will add to the number of social workers with interest and beginning expertise in practice beyond national borders. Strengthening of international associations and establishment of institutional affiliations will build the infrastructure of international social work and lead to a more confident and better prepared response to the realities of global interdependence in the 21st century.

SCOPE AND CONTENT OF THIS BOOK

Issues in International Social Work addresses the social work response to a number of key social, economic, and political issues that are global in scope and have a major effect on the quality of life of people around the world. Each issue is examined in depth, with an emphasis on those aspects that have particular implications for social work involvement and intervention; then the authors focus on the specific challenge for special work in the context of the larger issue.

James Midgley addresses social work's role in the field of international social development in the initial chapter. Midgley reviews the problem of global poverty and the importance of social development as a complement to economic development in the battle against poverty around the world. He considers the relevance of a social development perspective to social work practice and the opportunity for social work to adopt a social development strategy internationally.

Marie Hoff summarizes the key dimensions of the environmental crisis around the world and the effects of environmental decline on the quality of life. She reviews sustainable development as a global movement to provide a more functional approach to human interaction with the physical environment. Dr. Hoff argues that sustainable development is an important arena for social work and suggests ways in which the profession can effectively participate in the development of an environmentally and socially sustainable community around the world.

The globalization of economics has increasingly affected the quality of life in all parts of the world. Professor Antonin Wagner, an economist and social work educator, examines the emergence of the global economy and discusses its influence on the everyday life of ordinary citizens. He then looks at the implications of this trend for social work, including both limitations and possibilities for the social work role.

Changing demographics are a major reality in the world as we move into the 21st century. Janet George focuses attention on global "graying" and the challenges created by an aging population. Dr. George explores economic and political as well as social implications of a changing population profile and considers social services delivery needs in this context. She then gives attention to new roles for social workers, in particular the roles of supporting families and other caregivers of elderly people.

Lena Dominelli discusses feminism as a growing force throughout the world. She examines the development of feminist social work as part of this social movement and emphasizes the importance of global ties as a key factor in defining and explicating the role of feminism within the social work profession. Professor Dominelli argues that feminism should emphasize social development roles for social workers and should promote collaboration between women social workers in the developed and developing worlds.

The challenge of ethnic conflict and violence in the post–Cold War era is discussed by Vera Mehta. The author, a social worker who has served in UN peacekeeping and preventive diplomacy programs, reports on the global scenario of conflicts and the resulting toll of suffering. She explains UN efforts at preventive diplomacy and social development and then explores potential roles for social work. She places particular emphasis on challenges for social work education.

Ethnic conflict is the major cause of the global refugee crisis. Rodreck Mupedziswa discusses the extent and characteristics of this crisis and reviews the major refugee relief programs. He draws on his study of social work with refugees in Africa to examine a variety of roles for social workers in work with refugees. Finally, Mr. Mupedziswa discusses approaches needed to enhance the profession's involvement and effectiveness in the refugee field.

Social workers around the globe are active in both prevention and treatment programs directed at the HIV/AIDS pandemic. Ronald Mancoske considers HIV and AIDS as a global crisis and reviews social work contributions to international programs. Dr. Mancoske examines the social work response and makes recommendations about how the profession can more effectively use its expertise in epidemics across national borders.

In the final two chapters of the book, leaders of international associations examine the international role of the organized social work profession. Tom Johannesen, secretary general of IFSW, gives particular attention to his organization's role in the promotion of social justice and protection of human rights around the world. Ralph Garber, past president of IASSW, considers past development and current issues for social work education in the international arena. He places particular emphasis on the challenge of international standard setting for social work education.

REFERENCES

Chatterjee, P., & Hokenstad, M. C. (1997). Should the HBSE core curriculum include international theories, research and practice? In M. Bloom & W. Klein (Eds.), *Controversial issues in human behavior in the social environment* (pp. 185–198). Needham Heights, MA: Allyn & Bacon.

Frank, R. H., & Cook, P. J. (1995). *The winner-take-all society.* New York: Free Press.

Healy, L. M. (1995). International social welfare: Organizations and activities. In R. L. Edwards (Ed.-in-Chief), *Encyclopedia of social work* (19th ed., Vol. 2, pp. 1499–1510). Washington, DC: NASW Press.

Hokenstad, M. C., & Kendall, K. A. (1995). International social work education. In R. L. Edwards (Ed.-in-Chief), *Encyclopedia of social work* (19th ed., Vol. 2, pp. 1511–1520). Washington, DC: NASW Press.

Hokenstad, M. C., Khinduka, S. K., & Midgley, J. (1992). *Profiles in international social work.* Washington, DC: NASW Press.

Instituto del Tercer Mundo. (1997). *The world guide 1997/98: A view from the South.* Oxford, England: New Internationalist Publications.

Midgley, J. (1997). *Social welfare in global content.* Thousand Oaks, CA: Sage Publications.

Moynihan, D. P. (1993). *Padaemonium: Ethnicity in international politics.* New York: Oxford University Press.

United Nations. (1994). *World social situation in the 1990s.* New York: United National Department of Economic and Social Information and Policy Analysis.

United Nations Development Programme. (1996). *Human development report 1996.* New York: Oxford University Press.

2

Social Work and International Social Development

Promoting a Developmental Perspective in the Profession

JAMES MIDGLEY

The nations of the world have experienced unprecedented social progress during the 20th century. People today are better fed, healthier, and more educated than ever before. Throughout the world, life expectancy has increased, literacy rates have improved, and standards of living have risen. Of course, social progress has not taken place uniformly. There are many parts of the world where poverty and deprivation remain endemic, where women, children, and ethnic minorities are still oppressed, and where social conditions are appalling. However, the persistence of poverty and suffering in the modern world does not negate the conclusion that recent generations have enjoyed more prosperity than their ancestors could ever have imagined.

The idea of development is highly relevant to understanding the changes that have taken place. Many experts believe that industrialization, modernization, and economic growth have provided the impetus for progress. The idea of progress is closely related to the notion of economic growth (Arendt, 1978), but many experts also believe that economic growth is not of itself able to promote the well-being of the population as a whole. It is only when economic development is combined with social improvements that standards of living are raised. Required are policies and programs that enhance people's welfare and, at the same time, contribute positively to economic progress. In other words, social progress depends on the harmonization of economic and social development (Midgley, 1995).

The failure to harmonize economic and social policies has created a situation in many countries in which some people benefit from economic growth but the needs of many others are neglected. It has also created a situation in which social programs consume substantial resources without contributing to economic development. The current attack on the welfare state gives expression to the idea that social expenditures are a drain on the economy and inimical to continued economic growth. There is an urgent need to counter this attack by demonstrating that social policies can contribute to economic development in positive ways.

The integration of economic and social policies within a dynamic process of development is the essence of the developmental perspective. It requires that economic programs enhance social welfare and, conversely, that social programs contribute to economic development. Through an integrated approach of this kind, the well-being of people throughout the world can be improved.

Although this idea is not new, it is only in recent years that it has been articulated into a coherent model and has attracted widespread attention in social work. Social workers who have advocated the need for a developmental perspective are gaining more support. As social programs are being undermined by the radical right, developmental ideas offer a credible alternative to conservatives' attack on the welfare state. Growing interest in the developmental perspective has also been promoted by the 1995 United Nations World Summit on Social Development. The summit brought together many governments and voluntary organizations committed to improving global social conditions. Their commitment to international social development has given new impetus to developmental ideas and offers a fresh opportunity to harness the power of economic growth for social purposes on a global scale.

It is primarily at the international level in social work that the developmental approach has emerged and that efforts have been made to promote its unique perspective. This chapter describes the developmental perspective with reference to its historical evolution and key characteristics and discusses the role of social work in promoting a developmental approach. It also reviews previous attempts to identify developmental roles for the profession and suggests forms of intervention that foster this goal.

DEVELOPMENT AND UNDERDEVELOPMENT IN GLOBAL CONTEXT

The significant changes in social conditions that have occurred over recent decades are believed by many social scientists to be attributable to two factors: The first is economic growth, and the second is social intervention. The highest standards of living in the world today are found in those nations that experienced economic modernization and at the same time introduced extensive social programs. These countries are mainly in Western Europe, North America, Australasia, and the Far East. They transformed their impoverished agrarian subsistence economies into modern industrial societies and created mass wage employment, increased standards of living, and enhanced well-being for millions of people. However, government social welfare intervention also played a critical role in enhancing the standards of living. Governments intervened not only to promote economic development but also to improve social conditions through educational, housing, health care, income security, and other social programs. The combination of economic development with these kinds of social programs has formed the basis for prosperity in these nations.

Development has brought significant economic and social gains in these countries, but relatively few others have been able to harmonize the economic and social components of the development process in ways that ensure high levels of economic performance and enhance the social well-being of the population as a whole. Many nations have recorded high rates of economic growth without experiencing a concomitant degree of social progress. Although economic growth rates have been impressive in most parts of the world, levels of welfare have lagged (Loup, 1980; Morawetz, 1977), a situation sometimes referred to as "distorted development" (Midgley, 1995). Distorted development occurs through a mismatch between economic and social development. The problem in many countries is not an absence of economic development but rather a failure to harmonize economic and social objectives and to ensure that the benefits of economic progress reach the population as a whole.

Conditions of distorted development are widespread in the Third World. Perhaps the most dramatic examples has occurred in Latin America, where rates of economic growth have been impressive but where poverty and deprivation are endemic. Despite a significant degree of economic development, housing standards are inadequate, the distribution of income and wealth is highly skewed, investments in education and the social services are low, and rates of unemployment and underemployment are high. Similar examples are found in Africa and Asia, particularly in countries where economic prosperity has been achieved through exploiting natural resources. In these nations, mineral wealth has provided high standards of living for a small minority of the population but left the majority in conditions of poverty.

Distorted development also persists in industrial countries such as the United Kingdom and the United States despite their high level of economic development. In these countries significant sections of the population do not benefit from economic growth. Distorted development is manifested in high rates of poverty in decayed inner-city areas and deprived rural communities. Inner cities are increasingly devastated in both physical and social terms. Here poverty, unemployment, crime, family disintegration, violence, drug use, and social deprivation are most marked.

Distorted development is also manifested in the exclusion of sections of the population from full participation in development. Discrimination against members of ethnic and racial minorities prevents them from taking advantage of opportunities that can improve their standard of living. This problem is particularly acute for small groups of indigenous people, who are often isolated in remote regions or relegated to dismal reservations with few opportunities for advancement.

The oppression of women and the perpetuation of conditions of deprivation for hundreds of millions of women around the world are other instances of distorted development. Although women contribute to economic development, they seldom share its benefits equally. Their labor is critical to the rural economy, the urban informal sector, and increasingly, to the industrial and service sectors, but their incomes are lower than those of men, their status is inferior, and many live in conditions of deprivation and dependency. Another manifestation of the problem is the exploitation in many parts of the world of children who labor under grueling conditions and are excluded from educational opportunities, adequate health care, and a sense of security and well-being.

Distorted development is also manifested in environmental degradation. In many countries economic growth resulting from the exploitation of natural resources has benefited international corporations and local elites to a far greater extent than it has benefited local people. In addition, the environmental damage caused by these activities has harmed local communities and endangered the well-being of future generations.

THE DEVELOPMENTAL PERSPECTIVE

An integrated developmental perspective that effectively combines economic and social policies is needed to deal with these problems of distorted development. The developmental perspective also offers an alternative to the harsh policy prescriptions that continue to popularize the view that complete government disengagement from social welfare will create prosperity for all. Because the political right currently defines the terms of the debate on social policy issues, an alternative model that will appeal to voters and offer a viable alternative to outdated consumption-

and maintenance-oriented welfare programs is badly needed. Many social policy experts now believe that the developmental model offers an alternative of this kind.

The developmental perspective in social welfare seeks to promote the well-being or people through harmonizing economic and social policies within a dynamic process of development. It uses a comprehensive macro-perspective that focuses on communities and societies; emphasizes planned intervention; promotes a dynamic, change-oriented process that is inclusive and universalistic; and above all seeks to enhance people's welfare by integrating the economic and social dimensions of development.

History of the Developmental Perspective

The developmental perspective in social welfare emerged from the efforts of British colonial administrators in West Africa to identify forms of social welfare that would be compatible with the emphasis the colonial authorities placed on economic development (Midgley, 1994). In the 1940s, as the British government increased economic investments and the expansion of infrastructure in its colonies, remedial social welfare programs were given little priority. Because remedial social work catered primarily to juvenile offenders, beggars, and the urban destitute through the provision of residential and custodial services, it was often criticized for consuming scarce resources on unproductive activities (Livingston, 1969; Midgley, 1981). Faced with these criticisms, colonial welfare administrators sought to identify interventions that would transcend the remedial approach and contribute positively to economic growth.

An important innovation was the introduction of mass literacy, which not only involved conventional literacy training but also included such activities as small-scale agriculture and domestic animal husbandry; development of crafts and village technologies; construction of infrastructure such as feeder roads, bridges, and local irrigation systems; establishment of small family enterprises; improvement of community water supplies and sanitation; and building of health centers, schools, and other community facilities. These programs were designed to enhance the standard of living of ordinary people, particularly in rural areas. As mass literacy spread throughout the British Empire, a new term, "community development," emerged to describe these activities. This new term explicitly connoted a concern with development rather than remedial intervention and a focus on communities rather than individuals.

The contribution of the British government to social development was critical, but it was expanded and popularized by the United Nations (UN) and other international agencies. The UN adopted the term "social development" to convey its intention to transcend conventional remedial services and promote a wider developmental approach to social welfare (UN, 1971b). The idea that policies for economic growth needed to be closely integrated with social welfare policies was central to the organization's concept of social development. Leading economists such as Gunnar Myrdal, Hans Singer, and Benjamin Higgins were invited to recommend ways to achieve this. Criticizing the belief that economic growth automatically improves people's standards of living, they argued that governments needed to ensure that the benefits of economic growth reached ordinary people. They argued for the adoption of "unified socio-economic development planning" (UN, 1971b), and they recommended that government development–planning agencies intervene more actively to promote people's welfare. They also urged that social planners be recruited to implement policies that increased human capital formation, enhanced levels of living, and fostered the expansion of the social services.

After the implementation of these recommendations in the 1970s, social planning was widely adopted in the developing countries (UN, 1971b). Training courses for social planners were created, development–planning agencies employed more social planners, and national development plans gave more recognition to social programs and objectives (Conyers, 1982; Hardiman & Midgley, 1989). However, the UN was eventually criticized for promoting a top-down approach to social development that relied excessively on the intervention of the state. It was claimed that this approach neglected local communities and failed to involve local people in the development process. In response, the UN recommitted itself to community development and, during the 1970s, reformulated its community development ideas as "popular" or "community participation" (UN, 1971a, 1975). Other international agencies, such as the United Nations Children's Fund (UNICEF; 1982) and the World Health Organisation (WHO; 1982), also gave priority to community-based programs. As a result of these developments, community-based interventions are now regarded as a vital part of an overall social development strategy (Midgley, 1995).

The emergence of the developmental perspective was also supported by other development organizations. In the 1970s, under the leadership of Robert McNamara, the World Bank promoted a developmental approach that sought to integrate social and economic programs (World Bank, 1975). At about the same time, the International Labor Office urged its member states to approach the problems of unemployment and underemployment through an integrated development model. The basic-needs approach, which was adopted at the World Employment Conference in 1976, sought to ensure that policies for employment generation not only focused on economic aspects but placed emphasis on social welfare objectives as well (Streeten, Burki, Ul Haq, Hicks, & Stewart, 1981).

Although the developmental approach was pioneered in the developing countries, similar ideas may be found in some industrial nations, where governments have at various times sought to integrate economic and social policies. One example is the New Deal in the United States, which was introduced by President Franklin D. Roosevelt in the 1930s in response to the massive problems created by the Great Depression. The New Deal emphasized developmental programs that created social infrastructure and productive employment. Although it also introduced consumption-based programs such as Social Security and Aid to Families with Dependent Children, its emphasis on investment had a long-lasting effect. Perhaps the most impressive of its investment programs were the public works projects, which not only maintained people's incomes, reduced unemployment, and stimulated the economy, but also contributed substantially to the development of the nation's economic infrastructure. In the years between 1933 and 1943, a massive program to build schools, hospitals, museums, parks, stadiums, courthouses, airports, and other structures was implemented.

Another example of the use of a developmental approach in the industrial nations is the activist labor market and social policies of Sweden (Esping-Andersen, 1992). Rather than responding passively to social problems through consumption-based social programs, the well-being of the country's citizens is promoted through planned economic growth, employment generation, and a variety of social policies that integrate economic and social objectives. Sweden is one of the few industrial countries where the term "social development" is still widely used.

Features of a Developmental Strategy

The developmental approach seeks to harmonize social and economic interventions to promote a dynamic development process in three ways. First, it establishes organizational mechanisms to integrate economic and social policies. Although many developing countries have encouraged government economic development and social welfare agencies to work more closely together, this is not always the case and, in the industrial countries, it is rare. In addition, as a result of structural adjustment programs, the activities of many development–planning agencies in the Third

World have been curtailed. Social programs have also been retrenched in many parts of the developing world. The effective implementation of a developmental approach requires that social and economic agencies collaborate and integrate their efforts through improved coordination and planning, so steps must be taken to revitalize these agencies. Similarly, greater collaboration between economic development and social welfare agencies in the industrial nations is needed.

Second, the developmental approach requires economic growth to have a positive impact on people's welfare. There is little point in achieving economic development if the benefits of growth do not improve the lives of ordinary people. Unfortunately, there are many societies where economic growth has failed to foster real improvements in social well-being for the population as a whole. The problem of distorted development is widespread, particularly in Latin America and parts of Africa and Asia. It is particularly marked in societies where economic growth has failed to generate employment on a significant scale and where small groups of elites expropriate the nation's resources. It is particularly acute in mineral-wealthy economies and in societies where women and ethnic minorities are oppressed and excluded from sharing in the benefits of economic prosperity.

To remedy the problem of distorted development, proponents of the developmental approach urge the adoption of policies that ensure people's active participation in the economy. This can best be achieved through creating jobs and self-employment opportunities on a significant scale. It can also be fostered by removing entrenched racial and other discriminatory barriers to economic participation. Advocates of the developmental perspective also believe that national resources need to be judiciously redistributed to create social services programs that meet the basic social needs of all citizens. The notion of citizenship has no meaning if people do not have the opportunities to participate effectively in the economic life of their country. Proponents of the developmental approach contend that it is the responsibility of government to mobilize the major institutions of society, including the market and the community, to promote full participation and an equitable distribution of resources (Midgley, 1995).

Third, social development encourages the introduction of social programs that generate rates of return on social expenditures and contribute directly to economic development. Programs of this kind include services that promote the mobilization of human capital, enhance social capital formation, and increase opportunities for productive employment and self-employment among low-income and special-needs groups. These various productivist social welfare activities should be given priority over consumption-based services. Unlike traditional social welfare programs that allocate scarce resources to maintain needy people in unproductive and dependent situations, these programs generate returns on public expenditures and can be regarded as investments rather than outlays. Traditional social welfare programs are widely believed to detract from development efforts. However, productivist social welfare programs promote economic development and are potentially appealing to voters at a time when voters in many countries question the need for continued social expenditures on groups of people perceived to be dependent on the state.

PROMOTING A DEVELOPMENTAL PERSPECTIVE IN SOCIAL WORK

Social work is an internationally established profession. Schools of social work and professional associations exist not only in the Western industrial countries where the profession originated, but in the developing countries as well. Social work has distinct methods of intervention, an established knowledge base, and a defined set of values and ethics. Its practice methods use personal skills and apply scientific knowledge to promote human welfare. Although social work uses different forms of professional practice, it is primarily concerned with remedial intervention. The great majority of social workers practice with needy individuals and families who have personal problems arising from deprivation, neglect, abuse, and unsatisfactory social relationships. Most social workers are employed in agencies that specialize in the treatment of these problems, but in some countries, such as the United States, social workers also provide counseling to clients as private practitioners. Only a minority work in nonremedial settings such as community agencies that are concerned with the promotion of human welfare rather than the treatment of personal problems.

Social work's commitment to remedial practice has been criticized both within and outside the profession. Some believe that the remedial approach is a limiting and ineffective method for promoting human well-being. Others argue that social work's involvement in psychological counseling will undermine the profession's unique character (Specht & Courtney, 1994). If social work is to survive as a profession, it needs to transcend its narrow concern with remedial practice and promote activities that make a positive contribution to social well-being. Social work needs to reaffirm its historical commitment to eradicate poverty and promote human welfare in a positive sense instead of reacting to the personal problems of clients.

This criticism is particularly pertinent in view of the need for new ideas in social welfare that transcend conventional, remedial, consumption-based approaches. Social workers are frequently associated with outmoded welfare practices and are negatively perceived to be supporting a population of dependent clients who make little if any contribution to society. Until the profession is able to demonstrate that it can contribute to development, this negative public image is likely to persist. In addition, many critics have claimed that the problems of distorted development demand urgent social work attention. The profession's preoccupation with limited remedial interventions is, they believe, irrelevant to the most pressing problem facing humanity today.

An example of this attitude is to be found in the criticisms of social work in India by Bose (1993). He pointed out that the need for a developmental perspective in developing countries such as India is overwhelming. The incidence of poverty, problems of inadequate housing, prevalence of ill-health, oppression of women, and the country's many other social problems are so immense that social work's continued focus on remedial practice with families and individuals is completely inappropriate. Bose is particularly critical of India's schools of social work, which, be believes, do not prepare students to address the country's urgent need for development. The problem is compounded by the absence of well-developed professional associations that can link the profession to state and voluntary development efforts. Although the government of India has been committed to a developmental approach for many years, social work has not been a major contributor to these development efforts. Bose does not deny that the issue has been previously discussed in social work circles or that some exciting innovations involving social workers have been introduced. However, he argues that the profession needs to make a major commitment and radically change its conventional approach if it is to contribute positively to India's development efforts.

Another problem is that much of the profession's literature on development has failed to formulate a coherent approach that specifies in substantive terms what development social work entails. Much of the literature on the subject has been hortatory rather than prescriptive, and few social workers have a clear idea of how to implement developmental forms of social work. There is still much confusion about the definition of social development, and the literature has been so rhetorical and nebulous that it is difficult to translate these ideals into actual professional practice

(Lloyd, 1982; Lowe, 1995). Yet another problem is that many social workers have equated developmental social work with existing forms of professional practice, such as community organization and social planning. However, as Midgley (1995) pointed out, simply relabeling existing forms of professional intervention does not form an adequate basis for developmental social work practice.

TOWARD DEVELOPMENTAL SOCIAL WORK

Today, social work is challenged to make a major commitment to development. Although the literature on the subject is inadequate and there are problems in identifying developmentally relevant forms of practice, social work has been involved in the field for many years. As Midgley (1994) noted, social workers played a critical role in identifying the first developmental forms of intervention in colonial times, and American social workers have made a major contribution to articulating a theory for developmental forms of social work practice (Billups, 1994; Jones & Pandey, 1981; Meinert & Kohn, 1987; Sanders, 1982). The profession can undoubtedly contribute to the worldwide efforts currently under way to promote a developmental approach. Its long experience in working with deprived and needy people, global involvement, and ethical commitment to promoting human well-being suggest that a developmental approach is highly congenial to social work's historical role.

However, there is much more to be done. The social work profession must commit itself to the tasks and academic activities needed to support this initiative. Social workers also have to rethink existing ideas on a developmental social work. Current preoccupation in the literature with abstract and hortatory sentiments needs to be transcended by more tangible examples of how developmental social work can be formulated and implemented. To this end, Midgley (1995) has argued for a materialist approach to social development that offers concrete prescriptions for effective forms of developmental practice focused directly on incomes, standards of living, and other material components of social well-being. Although emotional needs and ideational issues need not be ignored, a material focus offers the best prospect for effective developmental practice.

The formulation of a developmental approach can also benefit from the experiences of colleagues in countries where developmental interventions have already been implemented. Social workers in different parts of the world, particularly the developing world, have formulated various forms of developmental practice that express a materialist commitment.

By learning from colleagues in these countries, social workers can greatly enhance their effectiveness (Midgley, 1990).

There are at least three ways in which social workers can promote a developmental approach. First, they can assist in the mobilization of human capital; second, they can foster the formation of social capital; and third, they can help low-income and special-needs clients engage in productive employment or self-employment. These different programmatic strategies foster a productivist approach to social welfare that transcends conventional remedial and maintenance-oriented services and integrates people into the economy. This approach not only increases the material welfare of social work's traditional clients but promotes economic development as well.

With reference to human capital formation, economists have demonstrated that investments in education, nutrition, and health care produce major economic gains. Much of the research has been undertaken in the field of education (Becker, 1964; Harbison, 1973; Schultz, 1963). Educational economists have shown that it is possible to quantify the rate of return to investments in education and to vary these investments to produce the highest rates of return on capital (Psacharopoulos, 1973, 1992). These analyses have shown that investments in primary education in developing countries produce higher rates of return than do investments in secondary and university education. Human capital studies have also been undertaken in health care and related services. This research has shown that investments in clean drinking water supplies, infant nutrition, and public health produce far higher rates of return than do investments in curative treatments and advanced medical technologies (Abel-Smith & Leiserson, 1978; World Bank, 1980, 1993).

Social workers can engage in programs that promote human capital development. For example, in many Asian countries social workers are actively involved in community-based programs that mobilize local people to establish day care centers to educate children and improve their nutritional standards. Parents and community leaders, with the support of social workers, use conventional community-organizing techniques to establish and operate these centers. Combining local involvement and state funds, they also offer maternal health education, family planning, and other programs to enhance the status of women. There is a good deal of evidence to show that investments in programs targeted at women produce net economic gains and contribute positively to development. The experience with community-based day care demonstrates that human capital programs are an effective way of engaging social workers in social development.

Social workers can also be involved in the formation of social capital. The concept of social capital is still poorly defined, but it is used to refer to the creation of cooperative networks and relationships in communities (Coleman, 1988). Putnam and his coworkers (1993) found that communities with well-developed civic traditions and dense social relationships experienced higher rates of economic development than those with low social integration. The term "social capital" also has been used to refer to the creation of economic and social infrastructure such as roads, bridges, irrigation and drinking water systems, clinics, schools, and other facilities (Midgley, 1995). These community-held assets are important because they provide the economic and social base on which development efforts depend. Another definition of social capital is based on Sherraden's (1991) work on social assets. Although his proposals focus primarily on individual asset accumulation through the creation of "individual development accounts," they are compatible with a developmental approach and are currently being implemented in various parts of the United States.

Social workers implementing a developmental approach can play a major role in promoting social capital formation. Their past engagement in community organization is highly relevant to the task. They have many years of experience fostering community activities, increasing participation, and strengthening community networks. Community organization also has been used in the past to mobilize communities to establish the social and economic infrastructure needed for development. Many Third World countries have extensive experience with community development programs that focus on social infrastructure development. Similar techniques can be used to promote social development in the industrial countries.

Social workers can also contribute to the implementation of a developmental perspective by helping clients engage in productive employment or self-employment. Social workers already have much experience in this field. Many routinely assist special-needs clients in enrolling in vocational rehabilitation and educational programs and finding employment. Social workers in many Third World countries have also been active in the creation of microenterprises for special-need and low-income clients (Balkin, 1989). This approach is now widely used in Asian countries such as the Philippines, where the government abolished its conventional cash social assistance program in the mid-1970s and replaced it with a microenterprise program (Reidy, 1981). Similar programs have been introduced in the United States, and, as Else and Raheim (1992) suggested, they offer a viable alternative to conventional income-maintenance programs that do little to restore low-income individuals to economic self-sufficiency or self-respect. It is likely that social workers in the industrial nations will become even more involved in microenterprise activities in the future.

As these examples reveal, social work can implement developmental forms of practice that transcend the profession's conventional, remedial, maintenance-oriented approaches and make a positive contribution to development. By adopting a developmental approach, social workers not only enhance the material welfare of needy people but also promote economic development. The forms of practice described in this chapter offer guidelines for promoting a developmental perspective in social work that has international relevance at a time when new ideas in social welfare are urgently needed.

REFERENCES

Abel-Smith, B., & Leiserson, A. (1978). *Poverty, development and health policy.* Geneva: World Health Organisation.

Arendt, H. W. (1978). *The rise and fall of economic growth: A study in contemporary thought.* Chicago: University of Chicago Press.

Balkin, S. (1989). *Self-employment for low-income people.* New York: Praeger.

Becker, G. (1964). *Human capital: A theoretical and empirical analysis with special reference to education.* New York: Columbia University Press.

Billups, J. (1994). The social development model as an organizing framework for social work practice. In R. G. Meinert, J. T. Pardeck, & W. P. Sullivan (Eds.), *Issues in social work: A critical analysis* (pp. 21–38). Westport, CT: Auburn House.

Bose, A. B. (1993). Social work in India: Development roles for a helping profession. In M. C. Hokenstad, S. K. Khinduka, & J. Midgley (Eds.), *Profiles in international social work* (pp. 71–84). Washington, DC: NASW Press.

Coleman, J. (1988). Social capital in the creation of human capital. *American Journal of Sociology, 94*(1), S95–S120.

Conyers, D. (1982). *An introduction to social planning in the Third World.* Chichester, England: John Wiley & Sons.

Else, J. F., & Raheim, S. (1992). AFDC clients as entrepreneurs: Self-employment offers an important option. *Public Welfare, 50*(4), 36–41.

Esping-Andersen, G. (1992). The making of a social democratic welfare state. In K. Misgeld, K. Molin, & K. Amark (Eds.), *Creating social democracy: A century of the Social Democratic Labor Party in Sweden* (pp. 35–66). University Park: State University of Pennsylvania Press.

Harbison, F. H. (1973). *Human resources as the wealth of nations.* London: Oxford University Press.

Hardiman, M., & Midgley, J. (1989). *The social dimensions of development: Social policy and planning in the Third World* (rev. ed.). Aldershot, England: Gower.

Jones, J., & Pandey, R. (Eds.). (1981). *Social development: Conceptual, methodological and policy issues.* New York: St. Martin's Press.

Livingston, A. (1969). *Social policy in developing countries.* London: Routledge & Kegan Paul.

Lloyd, G. A. (1982). Social development as a political philosophy. In D. S. Sanders (Ed.), *The development perspective in social work* (pp. 43–50). Manoa: University of Hawaii Press.

Loup, J. (1980). *Can the Third World survive?* Baltimore: Johns Hopkins University Press.

Lowe, G. R. (1995). Social development. In R. L. Edwards (Ed.-in-Chief), *Encyclopedia of social work* (19th ed., Vol. 3, pp. 2168–2172). Washington, DC: NASW Press.

Meinert, R. G., & Kohn, E. (1987). Towards operationalization of social development concepts. *Social Development Issues, 10*(3), 4–18.

Midgley, J. (1981). *Professional imperialism: Social work in the Third World.* London: Heinemann.

Midgley, J. (1990). International social work: Learning from the Third World. *Social Work, 35,* 295–301.

Midgley, J. (1994). Defining social development: Historical trends and conceptual formulations. *Social Development Issues, 16*(3), 3–19.

Midgley, J. (1995). *Social development: The developmental perspective in social welfare.* Thousand Oaks, CA: Sage Publications.

Morawetz, D. (1977). *Twenty-five years of economic development: 1950 to 1975.* Baltimore: Johns Hopkins University Press.

Psacharopoulos, G. (1973). *Returns to education: An international comparison.* Amsterdam: Elsevier.

Psacharopoulos, G. (1992). *Returns to investment in education: A global update.* Washington, DC: World Bank.

Putnam, R. D., Leonardi, R., & Nanetti, R. Y. (1993). *Making democracy work: Civic traditions in modern Italy.* Princeton, NJ: Princeton University Press.

Reidy, A. (1981). Welfarists in the market. *International Social Work, 24*(2), 36–46.

Sanders, D. S. (Ed.). (1982). *The development perspective in social work.* Manoa: University of Hawaii Press.

Schultz, T. W. (1963). *The economic value of education.* New York: Columbia University Press.

Sherraden, M. (1991). *Assets and the poor: A new American welfare policy.* Armonk, NY: M. E. Sharpe.

Specht, H., & Courtney, M. E. (1994). *Fallen angels: How social work has abandoned its mission.* New York: Free Press.

Streeten, P., Burki, S. J., Ul Haq, M., Hicks, N., & Stewart, F. (1981). *First things first: Meeting basic needs in developing countries.* New York: Oxford University Press.

United Kingdom, Colonial Office. (1954). *Social development in the British colonial territories.* London: Her Majesty's Stationery Office.

United Nations. (1971a). *Popular participation in development.* New York: Author.

United Nations. (1971b). Social policy and planning in national development. *International Social Development Review, 3*(1), 4–15.

United Nations. (1975). *Popular participation in decision making for development.* New York: Author.

United Nations Children's Fund. (1982). Popular participation in basic services: Lessons learned through UNICEF's experience. *Assignment Children, 59/60*(1), 121–132.

World Bank. (1975). *The assault on world poverty.* Baltimore: Johns Hopkins University Press.

World Bank. (1980). *Health: Sector policy paper.* Washington, DC: Author.

World Bank. (1993). *World development report, 1990: Investing in health.* Washington, DC: Author.

World Health Organisation. (1982). *Activities of the World Health Organisation in promoting community involvement for health development.* Geneva: Author.

3

Social Work, the Environment, and Sustainable Growth

MARIE D. HOFF

The unique strengths of the social work profession have been its emphasis on a holistic approach to the person and its development of practice methods that address the environment in which that person lives. In recent decades this person-in-environment approach has tended toward a narrowly specialized concern with the person's immediate social environment—the context of friends, family, and community that affects the person's functioning. Now the critical condition of the global physical environment is forcing all sectors of society, including the professions, to consider the implications of this crisis. An adequate social work response to the physical environment will demand a more holistic approach to practice through incorporation of the environmental, economic, and political dimensions of society, as has been suggested by the sustainable development movement.

The term "sustainable development" is widely used to describe the global movement to develop a more functional approach to human interaction with the physical environment. Theorists and activists agree that achievement of sustainable development will require profound shifts in most societies' environmental, economic, and cultural practices. Social work's traditional vision of a society that nurtures the development of all its members has much to contribute to this global agenda. However, members of the profession also have much to learn about the nature of this crisis and face extraordinary challenges and opportunities to participate in this critical global task in the next century. This chapter summarizes key dimensions of the global environmental crisis, describes the social trends and social and health problems and responses associated with the crisis, and proposes reconstructed theoretical perspectives, an expanded knowledge base, and new practice roles for social work.

GLOBAL DIMENSIONS OF ENVIRONMENTAL CRISIS

Human impact on degradation of the physical environment has two major dimensions: pollution and depletion. First, the basic components of soil, air, and water are being poisoned and polluted beyond the natural capacity of the planet to absorb and neutralize the contaminants. Pollution is caused by industrial, military, and consumer patterns of use and disposal of chemicals and other material resources. Second, water, air, soil, forest, and mineral resources are being depleted, and plant and animal species are becoming extinct at an extraordinary rate. Population increase and an energy system based on fossil fuels contribute to these processes. These twin dragons of pollution and depletion constitute an unprecedented human interference with the fundamental principles of ecological science—namely, that interdependence and diversity are essential to the self-regulating, self-sustaining capacity of the earth to maintain life (Commoner, 1971). Brown (1996, p. 18) stated, "The efforts now needed to reverse the environmental degradation of the planet and ensure a sustainable future for the next generation will require mobilization on a scale comparable to World War II."

Never before in history has human activity had the capacity to alter the basic chemical and climatic conditions of the planet. Scientists have accumulated sufficient evidence of global warming to garner agreement among world political leaders that the trend is real and that it portends grave and negative consequences for human society in the next century. Global warming already may be contributing to some of the extreme weather patterns—record-breaking hurricanes, droughts, and floods—occurring around the world. Population increase and intensifying economic pressures are leading more people to settle in the most disaster-prone areas. Slowly rising sea levels (from global warming and the thawing icecaps) may eventually destroy coastal and island ecologies and populations. Even more basic, however, is the effect of global warming on agriculture, particularly in the world's food basket, the temperate zones where the bulk of cereals are grown.

The rapid increase in global warming is caused by the effluents of modern industrial society, primarily carbon dioxide but also chlorofluorocarbons (CFCs) and nitrous oxide (Silver & DeFries, 1990), released into the air to form, in effect, a heat shield around the earth. Air pollution from the burning of fossil fuels also contributes to destruction of soil, the death of lakes and plants, and the corrosion of buildings, when acid rain returns these and other chemicals to the earth. Every continent is affected by acid rain, but soil composition in northern Europe and large sections of North America (for example, eastern Canada) renders some areas more vulnerable than others (Silver & DeFries, 1990).

Environmental Threats and Losses

WATER According to the United Nations (UN) 1994 estimate, the overall world supply of water per capita is only one-third of what it was in 1970. The UN (1994) also estimated that 1.3 billion people in the developing world lacked access to clean water in 1990, and nearly 2 billion lacked safe sanitation. Twenty-six water-scarce countries, primarily in Africa and the Middle East, which are listed by the Worldwatch Institute, a leading monitor of global environmental conditions, may face even further declines in water availability (up to 50 percent) by 2010 (Postel, 1993). In China, more than 82 million people in rural areas and residents in more than 300 Chinese cities find it difficult to procure water (Brown, 1995). Water is used up for agriculture and industry and polluted by chemical runoff and disposal. The Aral Sea, between Kazakhstan and Uzbekistan, is a leading example of a vast body of water drained by irrigation and poisoned by agricultural chemicals. The Aral Sea may be "the worst single instance of agricultural ecocide in the Soviet Union. . . . Two out of every three people examined in public health dispensaries are ill" (Feshbach & Friendly, 1992, p. 73). In Poland, only 3.4 percent of the water supply is classified as suitable for drinking or breeding certain fish (Bolan, 1994). People in the poorer nations of the world are threatened by water pollution from both untreated sewage and dumping of industrial wastes. Bacterial and viral diseases are spread through sewage-polluted waters, and chemical pollutants appear to be implicated in increasing rates of various forms of cancer. Even the vast oceans are overfished and seriously poisoned by human waste, threatening their capacity to sustain a major source of protein for human consumption (Weber, 1993).

SOIL Demand for land is a significant factor in social unrest and violence in many countries. The recent wars in Central America and the Zapatista uprising in Chiapas, Mexico, are based on a struggle to control land. In the United States, one of the greatest recent challenges to the authority of the federal government is the demand by states and private citizens for greater local control over public lands, which are a major economic resource for forestry and grazing of livestock. However, despite worldwide land scarcity, 6 million hectares of land become desert each year, and "29% of the earth's land area suffers slight, moderate or severe desertification" (World Commission on Environment and Development [WCED], 1987, p. 127). Land is desertified by poor agricultural and forestry practices that contribute to wind and water erosion. During the past 60 years, public works projects in every country around the globe, such as thousands of huge dam-building projects and highway construction projects, have also been major causes of soil loss (Rich, 1994). The world population explosion has also contributed to soil loss as impoverished rural populations migrate to cities and agricultural land is taken over for housing and industry. In the past 60 years, the world's rural population has doubled, but the urban population has increased tenfold, to around 1 billion (WCED, 1987). Lowe (1991, p. 14) described the situation: "[P]lanners in the Third World's giant cities face colossal environmental problems, from deadly air pollution in Mexico City, to indiscriminate dumping of toxic wastes in Alexandria, to the actual sinking of cities like Bangkok, Jakarta, and Shanghai from overdrawing of groundwater."

Soil loss and population increase have outflanked green technology affecting the world's capacity to feed people adequately. Every year, an estimated 13 to 18 million people, primarily children, die from hunger and related diseases (Bread for the World, Institute on Hunger and Development, 1995), and 786 million people face chronic hunger and malnourishment (UN, 1993).

AIR Global warming may be the ultimate threat to survival of life on earth. Although international protocols are contributing to a reduction in atmospheric CFCs, concentrations of carbon dioxide from burning of fossil fuels and deforestation continue to rise. Almost 6 billion tons of carbon dioxide are released into the atmosphere annually. The United States and Canada are the largest offenders, with 5.4 and 4.2 tons per capita, respectively, in 1992 (Roodman, 1994). Air pollution threatens the world's food supply because of its effects on plant life. More immediate effects include escalating rates of lung cancer, asthma, and other respiratory diseases. "Sixty percent of Calcutta's population suffer from pneumonia, bronchitis and other respiratory diseases related to air pollution" (WCED, 1987, p. 240). During the 1980s asthma increased in a number of countries. In the United States, where asthma increased 40 percent over the past decade, health researchers found that six of 10 asthma sufferers resided in urban areas where pollution levels exceeded air quality standards ("Asthma," 1995).

REDUCTIONS IN BIODIVERSITY The concept of ecology implies an interactive, interrelated set of components that vitally depend on one another for total continuity of the system. Diversity of living species is the linchpin of functional stability within this complex: Each species of plant and animal life depends on other species in the food chain, and each predator performs a vital function in keeping its prey within sustainable limits. Until now only the human species has been able to evade this fundamental law of ecology. Global warming, military activity, mining, agriculture, forestry, urban expansion, and numerous other human activities pose serious threats to ecological subsystems around the world, undermining the natural biodiversity and contributing to species extinction at a rate vastly greater than normal, evolutionary extinction rates. Deforestation alone accelerates species extinction to rates 10,000 times greater than is natural; tropical deforestation may result in the loss of 15 percent to 20 percent of all species by 2000 (Silver & DeFries, 1990).

Species diversity is defensible in ethical terms alone. However, species diversity is also absolutely vital to human survival. Surprising new health and medical uses of various species are routinely found. Industrialized agriculture, based on hybrid monocrops, reduces the diversity among food crops, which threatens the health of these crops (George, 1984, 1992; Shiva, 1991). Agricultural researchers are constantly in search of increasingly scarce wild varieties of major food crops to strengthen the crops' genetic strains. A major social justice and political issue between indigenous peoples and corporate researchers concerns the efforts of corporations to patent and obtain exclusive control over genetic resources. Farmers in India have staged huge protests against international trade agreements that could require them to pay royalties to save and reuse their own seed stocks. "What we are seeing is a blatant effort by a few corporations to establish monopoly control over the common biological heritage of the planet" (Korten, 1995, p. 180).

At this time in world history, it is difficult to overstate the seriousness of the condition of the planet. Organizations that monitor the global condition, such as the UN and the Worldwatch Institute, generally report rapidly deteriorating conditions by a wide variety of indicators. Beyond the staggering question of whether life in any form will be sustained beyond the next century is the question of the quality of life. Both well-off and poor people are besieged by toxic threats to air, water, and soil. Visual blight and deafening noise pollution in the world's megacities also diminish the quality of life. Many modern stress-related diseases, as well as escalating levels of violence around the world, are traceable to the indifferent abuse of the environmental foundations of human life.

Effects of Environmental Decline on Quality of Life

Diseases and developmental abnormalities are attributable to many factors, such as bacteria, viruses, genetic and hormonal disorders, and physical and mental stress. The disease-causing power of all these factors is exacerbated by a degraded environment. Some emerging data seem sensational, but they have profound implications, such as the recently reported 50 percent decline in human sperm count since 1940. But the widely used chemicals (including some in household detergents and plastics) that cause this abnormality also alter "a whole spectrum of morphological, physiological, reproductive, and life history traits. Tumors, deformities, reproductive abnormalities, and reduced survivorship are widespread in exposed fish, birds, and mammals" (Abramovitz, 1996, p. 73).

The paradoxical effect of technological innovations, including advances in medical science, is that science has improved the quality of human life and conquered some diseases such as smallpox, but science has also led to drug-resistant strains of bacteria and viruses. This outcome, combined with the explosion of megacities, has resulted in three-fourths of the world population being exposed to deadly infectious diseases (Platt, 1996), such as cholera, tuberculosis, hepatitis, diarrhea, and a variety of other airborne and waterborne killers. Almost 3 million children under age 5 die from diarrhea each year (Platt, 1996).

The 20th-century chemical revolution has added the most new threats to health of both people and animals. WCED (1987) reported an estimate of 10,000 deaths and 400,000 cases of acute reactions from pesticide poisoning in developing nations. At the Love Canal, New York, toxic waste site, 400 chemicals were found. "Documented effects from toxic exposure at Love Canal included statistically significant increases in fetal deaths, miscarriages, and birth defects, which included missing and deformed kidneys, webbed and extra toes, deafness, heart malformations, mental retardation, and Down's syndrome" (Rogge, 1994).

Billions of pounds of chemical wastes are released annually into the soil, water, and air to contribute to these and other documented diseases. Studies of the *maquiladoras* (workers in manufacturing assembly plants) living along the Mexico–United States border have found high incidence of low-birthweight babies, cancer, and mental retardation among the children of women who work in this highly polluted and uncontrolled region (Satchell, 1991). Radiation poisoning from nuclear energy and nuclear weapons production contributes to cancer, thyroid disease, mental retardation, and weakened immune systems (Lenssen, 1992). South Pacific islanders were severely affected by U.S. nuclear weapons testing during World War II (Thomas, 1995; U.S. House of Representatives, 1994); the Navajo people and their animals continue to suffer severe disease effects from mining of radioactive materials in the southwestern United States (Dawson, 1994); and radiation from the Chernobyl disaster in Ukraine may cause several hundred thousand deaths from cancer worldwide (Feshbach & Friendly, 1992; Lenssen, 1992).

The effects of environmental degradation on mental health are more difficult to prove directly. Toxins may produce such symptoms as irritability or reduced sexual drive. Stress and anxiety reactions result from living near waste sites, working in dangerous workplaces, and worry or grief over loved ones destroyed by man-made environmental disasters, such as the chemical spill in the Union Carbide plant in Bhopal, India, where more than 2,000 people died and some 200,000 more were severely disabled (Alvares, 1994; Morehouse & Suleramanian, 1986). Some public works projects, especially giant dams, displace hundreds of thousands of people and in doing so, destroy the foundations of mental health—human relationships, culture, and memory (Rich, 1994).

POPULATIONS FACING SPECIAL RISKS All people, and all other life on earth, have already been affected by the various assaults on the physical environment. Since the disruption of the ozone layer by CFCs, anyone who steps into the sun faces greater exposure to ultraviolet light. Members of the social work profession must become more informed about the social justice dimensions of environmental breakdown. Social work's traditional constituencies, children and poor people, suffer inordinate risk and damage from abusive treatment of the natural environment.

Children's developing bodies are more vulnerable to a wide variety of threats. In the United States, 44 percent of urban African American children are at risk of lead poisoning from paint in older buildings (Agency for Toxic Substances and Disease Registry, 1988; Truax, 1990). In countries where automobile emissions are uncontrolled, lead poisoning affects intelligence and neuromuscular development. In many parts of the world, children are exposed to agricultural pesticides and herbicides when they are cared for in the fields by their impoverished working parents. In some cases child workers themselves apply dangerous chemicals and are severely injured or killed in accidental overdoses. Moses (1993), a physician and founder of the Pesticide Information Center, has inventoried numerous studies from a number of countries that document the severe and wide-ranging illnesses and disabilities resulting from agricultural chemicals.

Members of minority ethnic groups and poor adult workers in agriculture, mining, and other dangerous industries, as well as people living in poor communities and poor nations (predominantly in Africa and the southern hemisphere, but also in China and the former Soviet Bloc countries) are also at special risk. Their disadvantage with respect to political, economic, and social powers renders these workers more vulnerable to exploitation in the most dangerous and unregulated industries, condemns them to live in the most polluted environments, and weakens their ability to resist the dumping of dangerous wastes in their local communities (Bolan, 1994; Bullard, 1993; Rich, 1994; Rogge, 1994).

Women play a distinctive role in the population explosion, which is a major issue in world environmental concerns. The environmental movement and the worldwide movement for women's rights have highlighted the significant disadvantages, injustices, and sheer abuse experienced by women in virtually every culture in the world. The 1994 UN conference on population held in Cairo resulted in a first-time worldwide agreement that improvement in the economic and social status of women is the necessary foundation of success in reducing world population (UN Children's Fund, 1995).

Social Trends and Issues Associated with Global Environmental Conditions

For most of human history, the physical environment was the unnoticed field or stage on which the forces of human culture, politics, and economy contended. Now environmental conditions are recognized as forces deeply influencing all aspects of human life, ranging from parents grieving over a malformed or dead child, to internecine struggles for access to land and water, to nations and corporations haggling over rights to fishing zones, dumping zones, or other resources. Environmental issues are directly related to a variety of social concerns: staggering rates of global poverty and unemployment, increasing rates of hunger and malnutrition (with the associated health and developmental deficits), escalating violence and war, record-breaking numbers of refugees and migrants around the world, health and social problems associated with growing urbanization in all parts of the globe, world population explosion and the family planning movement, and the worldwide human rights movement. Social and political activists are increasingly aware of the intrinsic connections among these many issues that have frequently been addressed separately in the past. There is a growing worldwide movement to link achievement of economic, environmental, and social development goals within the concept of sustainable development.

THE SUSTAINABLE DEVELOPMENT MOVEMENT: PRINCIPLES AND STRATEGIES

The sustainable development movement, insofar as it is a populist and democratic movement, asserts that the critical condition of the planet and the impoverishment and destitution of an increasing proportion of the world's population are rooted in a global economic system devoted to profit, growth, and monopolization of resources by fewer and fewer players—namely, the transnational corporations and the international financial systems that support them (Brecher & Costello, 1994; Danaher, 1994; Korten, 1995; Rich, 1994). The drive toward sustainable development represents an exponential leap in consciousness raising regarding the intricate ties between the global economic system and contemporary social issues, such as the condition of women, workers' rights, family and cultural survival, and ecology. In this process populist (that is, grassroots) proponents of sustainable development are also finding new ways to strengthen the political power of disadvantaged social groups, through building alliances and coalitions across identity groups, among the various sectors and levels of society, and across national boundaries. The strength of these new alliances can be inferred from the impact of NGOs on recent UN conferences, such as the 1992 environmental summit in Rio de Janeiro, the 1994 population conference in Cairo, the 1995 social development summit in Copenhagen, and the 1995 women's conference in Beijing. Sustainable development, as a concept and as an activist–populist movement, can be seen as the force that will gradually inform and transform cultural, political, economic, and scientific–technological thought and behavior in the 21st century.

"A country can cut down its forests, erode its soils, pollute its aquifers and hunt its wildlife and fisheries to extinction, but its measured income is not affected as these assets disappear. Impoverishment is taken for progress" (Repetto, 1992). Sustainability implies an approach to the use of material and natural resources that meets the immediate needs of the present generation and maintains the carrying capacity of the natural environment, preserving the common heritage of the planet for future generations (WCED, 1987).

In capitalist economics, development focuses primarily on the production of material wealth; capitalism in particular has been unwilling to question the distribution or the nature of the material wealth created. In contrast, the democratic sustainable development movement emphasizes that economic policy should give priority to production of resources for the basic needs of all people, rather than production of luxuries and amenities. It stresses that development goals also include measures of improved well-being beyond material wealth per se. These include improvements in literacy and health, as well as improvements in respect for basic human rights and participation by all people in their structures of governance. Sustainable development focuses as much on preservation and development of cultural institutions as on economic and material production, and it repudiates bottom-line commitment to growth, profit, and consumption as the primary goals of economic activity.

From this critique of economic purposes, sustainable development advocates use of new and more complex accounting systems to measure net improvements in wealth and social indicators, minus negative costs of crime, illness, and pollution and depletion of environmental resources (Brown, Flavin, & Postel, 1991; Daly & Cobb, 1989; Repetto, 1992). This contrasts with both gross domestic product accounting by government and corporate profit measures, which are greater when social and environmental costs can be externalized (that is, not paid for by the company). Germany, Norway, Sweden, France, The Netherlands, Canada, the Philippines, and Japan are working at developing accounting systems to incorporate natural resource depletion (Korten, 1995; Stead & Stead, 1992). The social work profession, with its long experience in measuring social problems and assessing social conditions, has much to contribute to the development of more sophisticated assessments of net improvements in the social condition of humanity.

Sustainable development is a highly political movement that challenges the distribution of power and wealth within individual societies, as well as the inequality between the industrialized and poor nations of the world. Extreme wealth and extreme poverty, for different reasons, are destructive of the natural environment. These inequalities also nurture social unrest and violence. To overcome these trends, sustainable development theory and practice insist on the democratization of all social institutions, including economic institutions, the workplace, and financial institutions (local, national, and international banking and credit organizations, notably the World Bank and the International Monetary Fund). The challenge in the next century will be to develop suitable structures and mechanisms to enhance democratized, decentralized decision making and to find feasible means to democratize the international governance structures that become ever more crucial as global interdependence intensifies (Boulding,

1988; Korten, 1995). The profession of planning (traditionally suspect because of its association with centralized state planning under Communism) can be expected to burgeon in the next century. As human populations urbanize and resources become ever more precious, careful deployment of planning skills will become more urgent. Such planning, already under way in many local and regional efforts, will be characterized by intersectoral, interprofessional cooperation among, for example, the social sciences and professions, biological and geographic sciences, urban planners and architects, artists, and most of all, the citizens whose lives and livelihoods are at stake. "The Copernican Revolution divided science and religion and initiated an awakening to the potentials of the material side of our existence. The Ecological Revolution now invites us to experience ourselves as spiritually alive and politically active participants in the unfolding exploration of a living universe" (Korten, 1995). In the 21st century, within a people- and environment-centered development paradigm, profoundly different values would be the basis for societal structures and processes. Private consumption and wealth accumulation goals would be subservient to values of communal sharing and simpler lifestyles for people who are well-off. Wherever possible, capital accumulation and machine-intensive technology would defer to labor-intensive technology to maximize employment and minimize negative environmental impact. Concern for growth and quantitative increase would be replaced by a concern for quality, equity of distribution, and safety and durability of products. It is particularly important to professionals in the field of social welfare that a sustainable development agenda operationalize political and economic policies and practices that demonstrate equality for women and that provide resources and sufficient time for employees' family life and their civic and cultural participation.

THE ROLE OF SOCIAL WORK IN ADDRESSING ENVIRONMENTAL AND SOCIAL SUSTAINABILITY

The social work profession has a role to play in the restoration of a viable physical environment and the development of the norms and practices to support sustainable societies. The profession's foundation in humanistic values and its articulation of the person-in-environment framework for theory and practice provides a solid base from which to build. However, substantial reorientation of theory, acquisition of new knowledge, and creative expansion and development of new practice roles are also necessary if social work is to be a serious participant in this life-and-death challenge to human civilization.

Theory and Knowledge for Social Work in Sustainable Development

As social work has developed, the person-in-environment framework has generally narrowed to a myopic focus on the social ecology of the client system. Moreover, systems theory, which is widely known and used in the profession, is inadequate because of its mechanistic orientation and inability to incorporate the organic and the spiritual dimensions of human existence. The ecological framework developed by Germain and Gitterman (1980) exhorted attention to the physical conditions of the client system but did not address or develop an understanding of the actual deterioration of the environment in every part of the globe, or of the equally deplorable effects on billions of people living in those conditions. A refinement of the ecological framework would require more than the course work in human biology or systems theory now commonly taught in professional schools of social work. Courses in ecological science are needed, as well as environmental studies that use interdisciplinary knowledge to deepen understanding of how human health and differing cultures are grounded in various ecosystems. An extensive body of research documents the wide range of health and social effects of environmental abuses, and this knowledge is essential to social work's ability to assess and respond adequately to those effects (Hoff & McNutt, 1994).

The environmental crisis has stimulated a degree of rapprochement between science and religion, as analysis of the roots of the environmental crisis has led many to a critical re-examination of the materialist values that drive exploitation and destruction on such a vast scale. The environmental issues discussed here cannot be addressed adequately in social work education and practice without a deepened integration of religious and spiritual concepts and values. Religion contributes to discovery of a heightened sense of limits and moral categories, recovery of a sense of the sacredness and poetry (mystery) of the earth, and a new emphasis on the spiritual values of human relationships, community, creativity, and altruism as dominant over materialist values of acquisition, consumption, power, and control (Berry, 1988).

Figure 3.1 shows the reconstruction of the person-in-environment framework that integrates the physical, environmental, and biological dimensions with the religious–spiritual dimensions.

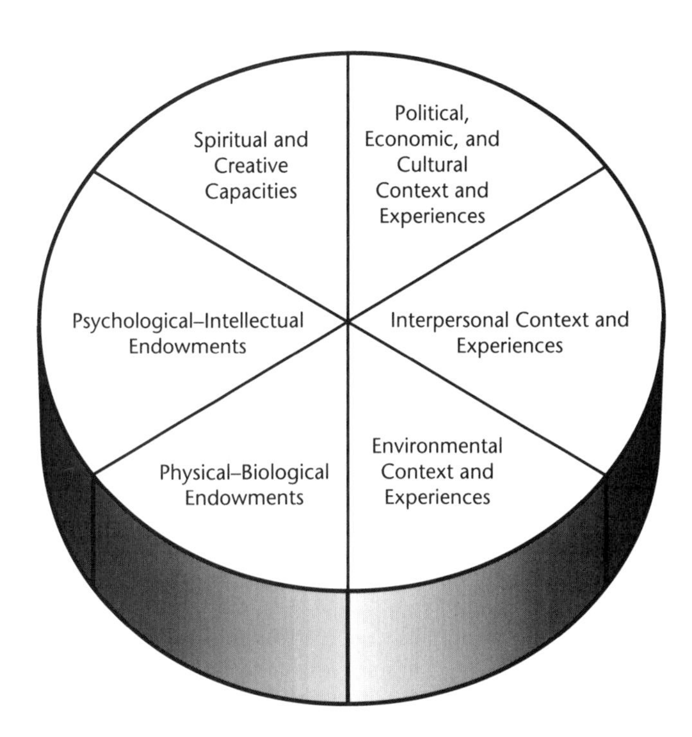

FIGURE 3.1 ***Reconstructed Person-in-Environment Framework***

McNutt and Austin (1990, March) and Midgley (1996) have noted the deficiency of economic knowledge within the social work profession. The discussion here of the reigning economic forces behind the stripping and poisoning of the planet should demonstrate that social work participation in debate over solutions will require a more sophisticated grasp of economic concepts. Any of the basic human needs—water, soil, housing, health care, and so forth—cannot be addressed without the ability to argue and conduct policy analysis in economic terms.

New Skills and Arenas for Social Work Practice

Many individual practitioners in many countries are already working to respond, with a range of research and intervention skills, to health and social problems that came from environmental causes (Hoff & McNutt, 1994). However, the profession's response is not systematic. Assessment and intervention protocols with client systems at the individual, family, and community levels, should be expanded to incorporate investigation of, and response to, environmental sources of ill health or social injustices. Conditions in the household (for example, cleaning or gardening chemicals, heating equipment); workplace contaminants or stressors; ratings of community soil, air, and water purity; proximity to toxic waste sites; and access to natural beauty and outdoor recreation (or lack thereof) are just a few of the environmental factors that must be understood to evaluate the sources of many contemporary dysfunctions.

Which skills are needed to respond to environmental problems? Crisis intervention and mental health treatment skills need refinement to include abilities for effective response to health needs and emotional distress of victims of weather and climatic disasters, people injured or displaced by toxic materials accidents, or refugees fleeing breakdown of local environments from war and technological disasters.

Social workers are challenged by the opportunity to participate in the sustainable development movement, through becoming actively involved with local experiments in various aspects of sustainable living and local and regional public planning, as well as through engagement with national policy-making and international social movements for human rights, social justice, and environmental restoration and protection. Social workers can use research studies in social development and community economic development to become familiar with promising new initiatives in sustainable provision of housing, food, health care services, and employment throughout the world. They can contribute a wide variety of skills and resources to these experimental approaches to basic needs.

Social workers should be the primary source of professional knowledge concerning the effects of public planning proposals on human needs and community relationships. In Hawaii, public policy requires social impact assessments for all development proposals, and social work practitioners have demonstrated their skills in conducting such analyses (Matsuoka & McGregor, 1994). Both as citizens and as representatives of social welfare organizations, social workers need to develop a more visible presence in housing, transportation, land use, facilities siting, and other public planning processes. Social work's skills in organizing groups can help to instigate such planning processes in communities where they do not currently exist.

At the national policy-making level, social work advocacy for institutional social welfare models (universal social security programs) can be strengthened by a refined analysis that incorporates knowledge gained from study of the environmental crisis—namely, that extremes of wealth and poverty not only degrade the environment but also exacerbate social violence. Advocates for environmental protection would gain political ground by paying more explicit attention to the human dimensions of the issues (such as poverty, unemployment, displacement, and racial and gender injustice). Social workers' policy analysis and advocacy positions, in turn, would be strengthened by incorporation of the environmental and economic dimensions of social issues and by alliance with environmental and workers' legislative lobbies.

The social work profession began with a zealous effort to improve the lives of children. Social work's agenda for its second century must incorporate and highlight the threats to future generations of children that are posed by the pervasive degradation of the natural environment. "The environmental abuse of children is as devastating and pervasive as the physical or emotional abuse" (Rogge & Darkwa, 1996). As with other collaborative approaches to analysis and advocacy, child advocacy around environmental threats does not constitute a new strategy but rather an incorporation of environmental causes of injustice and injury to children and expansion of the strategies for response.

As a new century and a new millennium approach, social work has a heightened opportunity to develop a new internationalism. Although the 21st century may seem to threaten environmental and social systems collapse, there is also a palpable new energy apparent around the world to confront the issues with new visions and collaborative strategies. Social workers can become more visible players in the international movement for human rights, which increasingly draws attention to the profound abuse of women and children around the world, most particularly in the economic arena. The human rights movement also has salience for social work's commitment to ethnic minority and indigenous people's needs. In November 1995, Nigeria executed Ken Saro-Wiwa for his unflagging fight against the oil production that is destroying the environment and the culture of the Ogoni people, a minority group in Nigeria. His murder and those of other environmental activists have stimulated awareness of the conjunction of human rights violations and environmental plundering (Sachs, 1996). Coalition building and strengthening of citizen-based, democratic alliances across boundaries of race, gender, nation, or issue of concern can be expected to grow stronger in the next century. Social work conferences, international associations, and political work will be significantly strengthened by efforts to cooperate with representatives from international social justice movements.

The environmental crisis has provided a new prism through which to view the hidden assumptions and values, latent power relationships, and destructive social patterns of the modern industrialized world. As the leading profession in the field of social welfare, social work has both a challenge and an opportunity to transform its approach to practice and participate effectively in the development of an environmentally and socially sustainable community around the world.

REFERENCES

Abramovitz, J. (1996). Sustaining freshwater ecosystems. In L. R. Brown (Ed.), *State of the world 1996: A Worldwatch Institute report on progress toward a sustainable society* (pp. 60–77). New York: W. W. Norton.

Agency for Toxic Substances and Disease Registry. (1988). *The nature and extent of lead poisoning in children in the United States: A report to Congress.* Atlanta: U.S. Department of Health and Human Services.

Alvares, C. (1994). *Science, development and violence: The revolt against modernity.* Delhi: Oxford University Press.

Asthma—United States, 1982–1992. (1995, January 6). *Morbidity and Mortality Weekly Report, 43*(51–52), 952–954

Berry, T. (1988). *The dream of the earth.* San Francisco: Sierra Club Books.

Bolan, R. S. (1994). Environmental quality and social welfare in Poland. In M. D. Hoff & J. G. McNutt (Eds.), *The global environmental crisis: Implications for social welfare and social work* (pp. 117–149). Aldershot, England: Ashgate.

Boulding, E. (1988). *Building a global civic culture: Education for an interdependent world.* Syracuse, NY: Syracuse University Press.

Bread for the World, Institute on Hunger and Development. (1995). *Hunger 1995: Causes of hunger.* Silver Spring, MD: Author.

Brecher, J., & Costello, T. (1994). *Global village or global pillage: Economic reconstruction from the bottom up.* Boston: South End Press.

Brown, L. R. (1995). Nature's limits. In L. R. Brown (Ed.), *State of the world 1995: A Worldwatch Institute report on progress toward a sustainable society* (pp. 3–20). New York: W. W. Norton.

Brown, L. R. (1996). The acceleration of history. In L. R. Brown (Ed.), *State of the world 1996: A Worldwatch Institute report on progress toward a sustainable society* (pp. 3–20). New York: W. W. Norton.

Brown, L. R., Flavin, C., & Postel, S. (1991). *Saving the planet: How to shape an environmentally sustainable global economy.* New York: W. W. Norton.

Bullard, R.D. (1993). Anatomy of environmental racism and the environmental justice movement. In R.D. Bullard (Ed.), *Confronting environmental racism: Voices from the grassroots* (pp. 15–39). Boston: South End Press.

Commoner, B. (1971). *The closing circle.* New York: Alfred A. Knopf.

Daly, H. E., & Cobb, J. B., Jr. (1989). *For the common good: Redirecting the economy toward community, the environment, and a sustainable future.* Boston: Beacon Press.

Danaher, K. (1994). *50 years is enough: The case against the World Bank and the International Monetary Fund.* Boston: South End Press.

Dawson, S. E. (1994). Navajo uranium workers and the environment: Technological disaster survival strategies. In M. D. Hoff & J. G. McNutt (Eds.), *The global environmental crisis: Implications for social welfare and social work* (pp. 150–169). Aldershot, England: Ashgate.

Feshbach, M., & Friendly, A., Jr. (1992). *Ecocide in the USSR: Health and nature under siege.* New York: Basic Books.

George, S. (1984). *Ill fares the land: Essays on food, hunger, and power.* Washington, DC: Institute for Policy Studies.

George, S. (1992). *A fate worse than debt.* New York: Grove Press.

Germain, C. B., & Gitterman, A. (1980). *The life model of social work practice.* New York: Columbia University Press.

Hoff, M. D., & McNutt, J. G. (Eds.). (1994). *The global environmental crisis: Implications for social welfare and social work.* Aldershot, England: Ashgate.

Korten, D. C. (1995). *When corporations rule the world.* West Hartford, CT: Kumarian Press and Berrett-Koehler.

Lenssen, N. (1992). Confronting nuclear waste. In L. R. Brown (Ed.), *State of the world 1992: A Worldwatch Institute report on progress toward a sustainable society* (pp. 46–65). New York: W. W. Norton.

Lowe, M. D. (1991). *Shaping cities: The environmental and human dimensions* (Worldwatch Paper No. 105). Washington, DC: Worldwatch Institute.

Matsuoka, J. K., & McGregor, D. P. (1994). Endangered culture: Hawaiians, nature and economic development. In M. D. Hoff & J. G. McNutt (Eds.), *The global environmental crisis: Implications for social welfare and social work* (pp. 100–116). Aldershot, England: Ashgate.

McNutt, J. G., & Austin, D. M. (1990, March). *Economics and social justice: Implications for the social work curriculum.* Paper presented at the 36th Annual Program Meeting of the Council on Social Work Education, Reno, NV.

Midgley, J. (1996). Involving social work in economic development. *International Social Work, 39,* 13–25.

Morehouse, W., & Suleramanian, M. A. (1986). *The Bhopal tragedy.* New York: Council for International and Public Affairs.

Moses, M. (1993). Farm workers and pesticides. In R. D. Bullard (Ed.), *Confronting environmental racism: Voices from the grassroots* (pp. 161–178). Boston: South End Press.

Platt, A. E. (1996). Confronting infectious diseases. In L. R. Brown (Ed.), *State of the world 1996: A Worldwatch Institute report on progress toward a sustainable society* (pp. 114–132). New York: W. W. Norton.

Postel, S. (1993). Facing water scarcity. In *State of the world 1993: A Worldwatch Institute report on progress toward a sustainable society* (pp. 22–41). New York: W. W. Norton.

Repetto, R. (1992). Accounting for environmental assets. *Scientific American, 266*(6), 94–100.

Rich, B. (1994). *Mortgaging the earth: The World Bank, environmental impoverishment and the crisis of development.* Boston: Beacon Press.

Rogge, M. E. (1994). Environmental injustice: Social welfare and toxic waste. In M. D. Hoff & J. G. McNutt (Eds.), *The Global environmental crisis: Implications for social welfare and social work* (pp. 53–74). Aldershot, England: Ashgate.

Rogge, M. E., & Darkwa, O. K. (1996). Poverty and the environment: An international perspective for social work. *International Social Work, 39,* 395–409.

Roodman, D. M. (1994). Atmospheric trends. In L. R Brown, H. Kane, & D. M. Roodman (Eds.), *Vital signs 1994: The trends that are shaping our future.* New York: W. W. Norton.

Sachs, A. (1996). Upholding human rights and environmental justice. In L. R. Brown (Ed.), *State of the world 1996: A Worldwatch Institute report on progress toward a sustainable society* (pp. 133–151). New York: W. W. Norton.

Satchell, M. (1991, May 6). Poisoning the border. *U.S. News and World Report,* pp. 33–41.

Shiva, V. (1991). *The violence of the green revolution: Third World agriculture, ecology and politics.* London: Zed Books.

Silver, C. S., & DeFries, R. S. (1990). *One earth, one future: Our changing global environment.* Washington, DC: National Academy of Sciences Press.

Stead, W. E., & Stead, J. G. (1992). *Management for a small planet: Strategic decision making and the environment.* Newbury Park, CA: Sage Publications.

Thomas, W. (1995). *Scorched earth: The military's assault on the environment.* Philadelphia: New Society Publishers.

Truax, H. (1990, January–February). Minorities at risk. *Environmental Action,* pp. 19–21.

United Nations. (1993). *Human development report 1993.* New York: Oxford University Press.

United Nations. (1994). *Human development report 1994.* New York: Oxford University Press.

United Nations Children's Fund. (1995). *The state of the world's children 1995.* New York: Oxford University Press.

U.S. House of Representatives. (1994). *Radiation exposure from Pacific nuclear tests.* (Oversight Hearing before the Subcommittee on Oversight and Investigations of the Committee on Natural Resources. 103rd Cong., 2nd Sess., February 24, 1994. Serial No. 103-68). Washington, DC: U.S. Government Printing Office.

Weber, P. (1993). *Abandoned seas: Reversing the decline of the oceans* (Worldwatch Paper No. 116). Washington, DC: Worldwatch Institute.

World Commission on Environment and Development. (1987). *Our common future.* Oxford, England: Oxford University Press.

4

Social Work and the Global Economy

Opportunities and Challenges

ANTONIN WAGNER

In recent times, the process of economic globalization has been affecting social cohesion within societies in many parts of the world. In a global economy social problems at the local level may be caused in part by economic changes occurring far away. This chapter discusses the local impact of economic globalization by assessing the risks of unemployment and earnings inequality for social cohesion. The situation in member countries of the Organisation for Economic Co-operation and Development (OECD) is emphasized, and the importance of community development as a classical social work strategy for both improving living conditions of ordinary people and empowering citizens at the local level is explored. Finally, building on the political philosophy of Hannah Arendt, the chapter discusses the role social work might play in times when the nation state is weakening and a global economy increasingly affects social cohesion in all societies.

LOCAL IMPACT OF A GLOBAL ECONOMY

As technology alters the nature of production processes and as trade expands, thereby intensifying competition, fundamental changes are taking place in modern societies. At the heart of this historic shift are capital-absorbing and labor-saving production technologies that reduce the need for human labor in industrial countries by replacing human beings in almost every manufacturing category. At the same time, competition forces companies to innovate and change production technologies to ensure that they are producing goods and services profitably. The globalization of economic activities and profound technological changes have brought on a fundamental transformation of the nature of human work.

Facing Labor Market Exclusion

During the next 25 years, many industrial countries will see the virtual elimination of the blue-collar assembly line worker from the production process. Until recently economists and politicians assumed that displaced factory workers would find new jobs in the service sector of their national economies. However, the service sector is beginning to be automated as well. In the banking and insurance sectors, companies are eliminating layer after layer of management and employees, replacing the traditional corporate pyramid and mass white-collar work forces with small, highly skilled professional work teams and using state-of-the-art software and telecommunications technologies. In the wholesale, retail, and catering sectors and in related industries, companies may continue to use large numbers of white-collar workers. However, they are being transferred from permanent jobs to short-term employment, including leased, temporary, and contingent work, in an effort to reduce wage and benefit packages, cut labor costs, and increase profit margins.

As a consequence of these developments, unemployment rates have remained at unusually high levels in industrial countries (Table 4.1). Throughout the OECD countries as a whole, employment grew just 1 percent in 1995. Although numbers vary considerably from country to country, unemployment in this group of the world's richest nations remains very high and, in some instances, it has recently been rising. In 1995 more than 33.5 million people in the OECD countries were unemployed, and the unemployment rate in the first half of 1996 was estimated to be 7.7 percent, compared with 7.6 percent in 1995 (OECD, 1996).

High unemployment throughout the OECD countries (and even rising unemployment rates in some European countries), along with the incidence of low-paid employment, are among the most important factors that have adversely affected personal income distribution in most countries since the mid-1980s. Social and political forces that have widened the disparity between rich and poor people in OECD countries were recently analyzed by the Luxembourg Income Study (LIS). Relying on the LIS database, a 1995 OECD report (Atkinson, Rainwater, & Smeeding, 1995) concluded that "personal income distribution, relative low incomes, and income inequality in general, are increasingly recognized as important economic and social policy matters in OECD countries—especially as they

TABLE 4.1 ***UNEMPLOYMENT IN OECD COUNTRIES***

OECD Countries and Regions	***Percentage of Labor Force***		***Millions***	
	1995	*Average, 1983–1993*	*1995*	*Average, 1983–1993*
North America	6.0	7.1	9.8	9.6
Japan	3.1	2.5	2.1	1.5
Western Europe	9.0	8.5	10.6	8.7
Southern Europe	12.6	10.8	8.7	6.9
Northern Europe	9.7	5.6	1.2	0.6
Oceania	8.2	8.2	0.9	0.7
OECD Europe	10.3	9.1	20.5	16.2
European Community	11.2	9.5	18.4	14.6
Total OECD	**7.6**	**7.3**	**33.2**	**28.0**

SOURCE: Organisation for Economic Co-operation and Development (OECD). (1996, July). *Employment outlook July 1996.* Paris: Author.

become more interdependent." As for countries outside the OECD, a United Nations survey published in 1996 found that the wealthiest and poorest people—both within and among countries—are increasingly living in separate worlds (Crossette, 1996).

These findings concerning personal income distribution have been corroborated by a recent study on trends in earnings dispersion in OECD countries (OECD, 1996), shown in Table 4.2. The study indicates that the broad trend toward rising inequality throughout these countries has continued since the early 1990s and has even spread to countries that maintained a stable income distribution during the 1980s. The United Kingdom and the United States have experienced an especially rapid rise in inequality, and only a few countries (notably Canada, Finland, and Germany) show a decline in earnings dispersion over the last 5 to 10 years. In some countries, a rise in earnings inequalities has implied a fall, or only weak growth, in real wages during the past decade for most jobs held by men in the bottom half of the earnings distribution (OECD, 1996). As a general rule, in countries where unemployment has been reduced successfully by transferring workers from permanent jobs to leased, temporary, and contingent work, earnings inequality has increased substantially because of the resulting wage squeeze. Conversely, in countries where systems of social protection in general and unemployment insurance in particular have prevented a further increase of earnings dispersion, unemployment has either risen or has not diminished significantly.

TABLE 4.2 ***TRENDS IN EARNINGS DISPERSION IN SELECTED OECD MEMBER COUNTRIES***

	Year			Change in Dispersion Measure	
Member Country	*1990*	*1993*	*1995*	*1979–1989*	*Since 1989*
Austria	1.80	1.79	..	0.02	0.00
Belgium	1.60	1.57	..	..	–0.05
Canada	1.85	1.82	..	0.03	–0.01
Denmark	1.57	..	..	–0.01	..
Finland	1.70	1.65	..	0.03	–0.02
France	1.99	1.99	..	0.02	0.01
Germany	1.64	1.61	..	0.01	–0.03
Italy	..	1.60	..	–0.03	0.19
Sweden	1.52	1.59	..	0.02	0.03
Switzerland	..	1.67	1.71	..	0.03
United Kingdom	1.84	1.86	1.87	0.09	0.03
United States[a]	..	2.03	2.10	0.12	0.06

NOTE: If not otherwise specified, dispersion is defined as the upper earnings limit of the 9th decile in proportion of the upper earning limit of the 5th decile. ·· indicates no data available.

SOURCE: Organisation for Economic Co-operation and Development (OECD). (1996, July). *Employment Outlook July 1996.* Paris: OECD.

[a] Males only.

Embracing the Corporate Economic Agenda

In a world that has turned into a global marketplace, growing competition and technological innovations lead to increased productivity on the one hand and a diminishing need for mass labor on the other. In these circumstances, economic growth, so much praised by the liberal agenda of the 1960s, has lost its positive effect on the living standard of working class people. Contrary to a famous metaphor, the rising tide does not lift all the boats anymore but lifts only the yachts of the rich. It is not corroding values but soaring unemployment as well as the general wage squeeze—and the confrontational strategy underlying it—that account for most of the notorious economic and social problems in many industrial countries (Gordon, 1996). Falling real wages and job insecurity are lurking behind the host of social maladies that plague our societies, including family breakdown, welfare dependency, and teenage pregnancy.

The impact of globalization on the everyday life of ordinary citizens is being felt all the more as the modern welfare state runs out of steam.

Mainly for fiscal reasons, governments all over the world have given up plans to temper negative side effects of economic development and engage in social spending. In response to budget deficits, fiscal authorities turn to a politics of austerity aimed at reducing domestic discretionary spending. Pension schemes, welfare payments, and health care subsidies are the most likely targets for budget cuts. At the same time there are no new resources for reviving the cities, providing decent housing to low-income families, and guaranteeing medical care to children and senior citizens. Not surprisingly, the poorest people suffer the most under these austerity measures.

Governments are debating what gets cut rather than what gets done, and they tend to embrace a corporate economic agenda that is supposed to refuel the economy and provide the necessary growth: lower taxes on the rich and corporations, deregulation, tight money, and cuts in pension benefits for employees. Using Congressional Budget Office numbers, the Center on Budget and Policy Priorities estimates that in the United States alone "corporate welfare" in the form of subsidies and tax breaks will cost taxpayers more than $722 billion over the next seven years (Borosage, 1996). Given the desperate fiscal situation of many countries, less revenue means less public spending, which will result in an abandonment of the welfare state and consequent punishment of poor people.

SOCIAL WORK AND LOCAL EMPOWERMENT

It is clear that a serious fiscal situation is faced by many member countries of the OECD. General government gross debt for the OECD countries as a whole reached some 65 percent of gross domestic product (GDP) in 1993, compared with about 40 percent in 1979, and debt ratios are currently rising in nearly all OECD countries (Leibfritz, Roseveare, & van den Noord, 1994). The question, however, is whether balancing the budget requires cuts in funding for social welfare, education, and housing, or whether there are workable alternatives in a time of austerity.

The European Model of Social Government

In the post–World War II period, European countries developed the European model of social government, which is quite different from the American understanding of how government works. According to the European model, governments were responsible for generous welfare spending and protective labor legislation. For decades many European governments also played a leading role as employer, regulator, and provider of

TABLE 4.3 ***MAASTRICHT CRITERIA: 1996 PROJECTIONS***

Country	*Inflation (April 1996), %*	*Public Deficit as % of GDP*	*Public Debt as % of GDP*
Austria	1.8	4.6	72.4
Belgium	2.1	3.0	132.2
Denmark	2.0	0.9	71.0
Finland	0.7	3.3	62.5
France	2.4	4.4	56.0
Germany	1.5	4.0	61.5
Greece	9.2	8.1	111.8
Ireland	2.0	2.0	81.3
Italy	4.5	6.2	122.0
Luxembourg	1.5	0.7	6.2
Portugal	2.9	4.6	72.0
Spain	3.5	4.6	65.0
Sweden	1.3	5.2	79.6
The Netherlands	2.0	3.5	79.4
United Kingdom	2.4	4.4	55.5
Maastricht Target	2.7	3.0	60.0

NOTE: GDP = gross domestic product.

SOURCE: Kamm, T., & Rohwedder, C. (1996, July 30). Many Europeans fear cuts in social benefits in one-currency plan. *Wall Street Journal,* pp. 1, 8. Reprinted by permission of *Wall Street Journal,* ©1996 Dow Jones & Company, Inc. All rights reserved worldwide.

public services. However, the Maastricht Treaty of 1991, which lays out the framework for a single currency in Europe (planned for 1999), has considerably affected the way European governments are functioning (Table 4.3). As the 1997 deadline for deciding who will join the European Monetary Union (EMU) draws near, European Union nations are seeking to meet the Maastricht criteria for joining the one-currency plan. By imposing strict budgetary criteria as well as debt and inflation ceilings on member states, the EMU forces governments to cast aside their generous postwar model of social government and adopt a socially regressive model similar to the U.S. system. Since the mid-1990s, the EMU has been acting among European countries as a catalyst for social spending cutbacks and other unpopular austerity measures.

Under the austerity politics triggered by the Maastricht Treaty, more and more European governments are shifting from the national to the local level at least some of the programs needed to temper the negative impact of globalization, technological changes, and deregulation on ordinary citizens' daily lives. Even in Europe, where it was deeply entrenched, the concept of state-centered welfare has eroded and given way to the notion of society as a pluralistic system in which the institutional blend of municipalities, local nonprofit organizations, and community-based trade unions complements the government in its formerly dominant role. In times when national governments are more and more compromised by succumbing to corporate demands, these local institutions are seen by many as a countervailing force against the overwhelming impact of the global economy on income distribution and the labor market. Therefore, area-based approaches to social policy become an important ingredient of the European welfare state. Welfare is more and more understood as "territorial" in character (Wagner, 1995).

The Principle of Territoriality

The principle of territoriality of welfare (and area-based approaches to social policy at large) emphasizes the solidarity and mutuality on which a local community of residence is built. Throughout the European Community (EC; today known as the European Union [EU]), area-based approaches to social policy were put in place long before governments decided to respond to budget deficits by shifting welfare spending to the local level. In 1975 the Council of Ministers initiated the First EC Programme to Combat Poverty (Weaver, 1988), which was a major cooperative effort among and within EC member states in the fight against poverty. With its decision of December 19, 1984, the Council of Ministers paved the way for the Second EC Programme to Combat Poverty, which ran from the end of 1985 until 1990. It included 91 action research projects that carried out at the local level new services and supportive activities for the benefit of poor people in local communities (Weaver, 1988). The Third European Programme to Combat Poverty began in 1990 and concluded in 1994. It included strategies based on a partnership between municipal agencies and private organizations and emphasized that area-based approaches involving citizen organizations and community groups are essential if the complex range of cumulative social problems resulting from a global economy is to be tackled (Frazer, 1995).

The EU's policy emphasis on local development and its enthusiasm for partnerships among public authorities, private enterprises and the voluntary sector, particularly locally based community organizations, builds on traditional social work strategies. In seeking answers to economic and social problems, local empowerment—grassroots, community-based, bottom-up initiatives that involve the local community—represents a more cost-effective use of resources than do traditional top-down programs. These initiatives can trigger financial revenues from other than public sources by linking politics of local economic development to politics of local social and community development. Moreover, dynamic blending of public and private forms of action with self-help and mutual support enables local empowerment strategies to mobilize the energies of marginalized, unemployed people and contribute to the development of vital human resources.

Despite its potential effectiveness, empowerment also has many limitations from a social work perspective. An important lesson to be drawn from the EC poverty programs is that area-based approaches can be severely inhibited by the lack of finances (Williamson, 1996). The success of local empowerment depends heavily on the involvement of a fiscally sound welfare state, and local initiatives should therefore be imbedded in an overall national strategy. As has been shown elsewhere (Wagner, 1995), the principle of territoriality of welfare has to be enhanced by the principle of universal coverage and the principle of adequacy in benefit levels.

It is important that all local communities within a given state be endowed with the necessary fiscal resources to cope with poverty and unemployment in their local territory. This requires adequate instruments of fiscal equalization on the federal or state level and an appropriate tax system on the local level. Because income taxes constitute a very important and flexible source of revenue, local governments should have access to such taxes. It is all too evident that many of the cumulative social problems in U.S. inner cities result from the tax system in operation at the local level. It forces central cities to tax their residents more heavily than do the suburbs, thereby creating an incentive for more affluent residents to leave the city. Only federal and state taxing powers with broad jurisdiction can compel suburbanites to pay significant shares of the cost, occurring mostly for core cities, of coping with urban poverty. Therefore, an efficient system of revenue sharing among the different levels of government becomes an important precondition for enacting area-based approaches to social policy.

SOCIAL WORK AS POLITICAL ACTION

In a global economy, professional social work in general and local empowerment in particular cannot be reduced to designing welfare programs and delivering social services at the local level. It is crucial for the future of the profession that social work become more attentive to the structural—and therefore political—issues involved at the national level and now also at the global level. What is the role to be played by social workers at the advent of modernity, a new and yet unknown age when the nation state is weakening and a global economy is increasingly affecting social cohesion in societies all over the world?

The concept of modernity owes much to the ideas of Hannah Arendt's *The Human Condition* (1958/1989). Although published almost 40 years ago, her study offers a startling and penetrating analysis of the state of humanity in the age of a global economy. Arendt's interpretation of modernity focuses on the concept of the social and builds on the theory of *vita activa* (fundamental human activities), distinguishing action (in Greek, *praxis*) from fabrication or work (in Greek, *poiesis*) and labor or life itself. It provides an excellent framework for rethinking the role in modern society of a profession designated by exactly the two Arendtian terms of "social" and "work."

The Rise of Social Concept and the Decline of Political Action

The concept of the social plays a crucial role in Arendt's assessment of modernity. She identifies the social with all those activities formerly restricted to the "shadowy interior of the household" (Arendt, 1958/1989, p. 38) or the private sphere. The social is the realm of biological and material necessity, of the reproduction of our condition of existence. Arendt claims that with the tremendous expansion of the economy from the end of the 18th century, these activities have taken over the public realm and transformed it into a sphere for the satisfaction of our material needs. The social realm (or society) has thus invaded and conquered the public realm, turning it into a function of what previously were private needs and concerns. The rise of the social has thereby blurred or even destroyed the boundary separating the public and the private. Obsessed with life, productivity, and consumption, we have turned into a society of jobholders and consumers who no longer appreciate the value associated with political life (Passerin d'Entrèves, 1994).

In conjunction with the concept of the social, Arendt introduced the tripartite division of fundamental human activities or conditions of "being-in-the-world": labor, work, and action. "Labor" designates activities catering to our biological needs of consumption and reproduction and thereby sustaining human life. "Work" alludes to the ability of human beings to build and maintain a world fit for human use and human enjoyment.

Work therefore provides an "artificial" world of things (artifacts), which is distinctly different from all natural surroundings (Arendt, 1958/1989). "Action" denotes the ability of human beings to disclose their identity, actualize their capacity for freedom, and endow their existence with meaning. Arendt claims that with the expansion of the social realm and the destruction of the boundary separating the public and the private, the distinctions among labor, work, and action are becoming meaningless, because every human effort is now expended on reproducing our material conditions of existence.

By distinguishing action (*praxis*) from work or fabrication (*poiesis*) and by linking action to freedom and plurality, Arendt has articulated a conception of politics in which questions of meaning, identity, and value can be addressed. Moreover, by viewing action as a mode of human togetherness based on equality and solidarity and connected to speech and remembrance, Arendt has offered a conception of participatory democracy that stands in direct contrast to the elitist forms of political representation and the bureaucratized welfare state so characteristic of the modern age (Passerin d'Entrèves, 1994). Arendt's conception of politics is based on the idea of active citizenship and the value and importance of civic engagement and collective deliberation about all matters affecting the political community. This conception of politics is in the classical tradition of civic republicanism that originated with Aristotle and is embodied in the writings of Jefferson and Tocqueville. According to this tradition, politics finds its authentic expression whenever citizens gather together in a public space to deliberate and decide about matters of collective concern (Passerin d'Entrèves, 1994).

Social Work in a Global Economy

How does Arendt's political philosophy help define the role of social work in a global economy? One may claim that Arendt's characterization of the social is somewhat elusive or overly restricted. By identifying the social with the activities of the household and by insisting on a strict separation between the private and the public, Arendt maintained that all questions pertaining to the economy are prepolitical or, even worse, apolitical. Thus, Arendt was unable to recognize that modern capitalist economies with the now-global market constitute a structure of power and a means of exploitation. By redrawing the boundaries between the public and the private, and by acknowledging that concerns for the social cannot be separated from the political sphere, social work, however, has the power to contribute to what one day may become the most important achievement of modernity—that is, the extension of social and economic rights to the underprivileged and least fortunate members of our societies. The principles of the United Nations General Assembly's *Universal Declaration of Human Rights* (1949) can be realized only if there is public sentiment in support of human rights in general and of economic, cultural, and social rights in particular. Social work practice and social work education could play a pivotal role in advancing what has come to be known as a "human rights culture."

Arendt's theory of action teaches a powerful lesson to the social work profession in a more straightforward way. Whereas work constitutes a mere fabrication of things (goods or services), Arendt pointed out that action constitutes a mode of human togetherness in which individuals are able to establish relations of reciprocity and solidarity. Action typically aims at establishing communicative relations based on mutuality, symmetry, and persuasion, not merely at producing services, whether social or personal in nature. There is a tension between the conception of social work as a services-rendering profession and this idea of political action. Action is characterized by the sharing of words and deeds, by processes of collective deliberation and mutual accommodation, not by delivering services, and even less by handing out food stamps.

CONCLUSION

More and more countries are experiencing the unsettling paradox that the process of economic globalization and rapid industrial expansion has increased general prosperity but also created growing numbers of unemployed and poor people. It is all too evident that the world economy increasingly affects social cohesion at the local level. The answer to mitigating the effects of long-term unemployment, labor insecurity, and low income—the main flaws of a global economy—may well be local empowerment or area-based strategies for securing the welfare of citizens. The aim of community development and related social work strategies should be to strengthen the bonds of local and functional communities as autonomous but interdependent parts of a global society.

Building on Hannah Arendt's political philosophy and theory of action, local empowerment and local action can go beyond rendering services, and social work can be understood as political action, thus providing the basis for a politics of solidarity and mutuality. The idea that the local community should be considered as a countervailing force to a global economy is also evoked by the concept of the *polis,* the Greek city–state.

Polis is an important Arendtian metaphor, and it stands for all those instances in history when a public realm of action and speech was set up among a community of free and equal citizens. In this respect *polis* could be said to epitomize the commons in a global world.

REFERENCES

Arendt, H. (1958/1989). *The human condition*. Chicago: University of Chicago Press.

Atkinson, A. B., Rainwater, L., & Smeeding T. S. (1995). *Income distribution in OECD countries. Evidence from the Luxembourg Income Study.* Paris: Organisation for Economic Co-operation and Development.

Borosage, R. L. (1996). The politics of austerity. *Nation, 262*(21), 22–24.

Crossette, B. (1996, July 15). U.N. survey finds world rich-poor gap widening. *New York Times,* p. A3.

Frazer, H. (1995). The European Union poverty programmes: An Irish perspective. In *Putting Poverty 3 into policy. Proceedings of a conference held in Ballyconnell, County Cavan.* Dublin, Ireland: Department of Social Welfare.

Gordon, D. M. (1996). *Fat and mean: The corporate squeeze of working Americans and the "myth" of managerial "downsizing."* New York: Free Press.

Kamm, T., & Rohwedder, C. (1996, July 30). Many Europeans fear cuts in social benefits in one-currency plan. In *Wall Street Journal,* pp. 1, 8.

Leibfritz, W., Roseveare, D., & van den Noord, P. (1994). *Fiscal policy, government debt and economic performance.* Paris: Organisation for Economic Co-operation and Development.

Organisation for Economic Co-operation and Development. (1996, July). *Employment outlook July 1996.* Paris: Author.

Passerin d'Entrèves, M. (1994). *The political philosophy of Hannah Arendt.* London: Routledge.

United Nations General Assembly. (1949). *Universal declaration of human rights.* Lake Success, NY: United Nations Department of Public Information.

Wagner, A. (1995). Reassessing welfare capitalism: Community-based approaches to social policy in Switzerland and the United States. *Journal of Community Practice, 2*(3), 45–63.

Weaver, S. J. (1988). *The Second EC Programme to Combat Poverty.* Cologne, Germany: ISG Sozialforschung und Gesellschaftspolitik.

Williamson, A. P. (1996, July 18–21). *Citizen participation, local social and economic development and the third sector: The influence of the European Union on policy innovation in the two parts of Ireland.* Paper presented at the Second International Conference of the International Society for Third-Sector Research, Mexico City.

5

Global Graying

What Role for Social Work?

JANET GEORGE

The "graying" of populations is a global phenomenon that affects the smallest Pacific islands as well as the most developed welfare states. Although graying is a global phenomenon insofar as official statistics can be deemed facts, it is debatable whether it constitutes a problem because aging, as with other social categories, is largely socially constructed and defined in relation to ideology, power, and structural arrangements. Aging is a proper subject for social policy analysis, with ramifications for social work intervention. However, in light of definitional issues and the diversity of older people, the usefulness of age as a policy-making category is increasingly questioned.

Social work has a long history of involvement with older people, from the days when they were defined as needy, not because of age but because of illness or inability to work. In those circumstances, without family support, they were subject to Poor Law or similar residual welfare. Now social workers are involved in the care of older people in a range of roles and services in health and welfare, including most recently, case management. This chapter explores the impact of global graying across developed and developing societies; it considers the way in which graying is constituted as a problem and outlines the current issues for older people, caregivers, and the wider society. The chapter also analyzes the effects on social work and the implications for social work education and practice based in a social development approach.

GLOBAL GRAYING: FACTS AND PERCEPTIONS

Data on demographic change indicate that reduction in both fertility and mortality rates is occurring worldwide, albeit to different degrees. The World Bank (1993) notes that Southeast Asian and Latin American countries have experienced rapid declines in both, whereas most sub-Saharan African and Middle Eastern countries have seen only minor changes, with both mortality and fertility remaining at high levels. The more developed countries of Europe, North America, and Asia, which achieved lower rates of fertility and mortality earlier, now have a more gradual rate of demographic change. The lower fertility rates and the lower mortality rates at older ages result in a rising proportion of people age 65 and older in all regions. This proportion of the global population is expected to increase from 7 percent in 2000 to 10 percent in 2025.

These general figures mask the variation between developed and developing countries. In developed countries, people age 65 and older are expected to make up 20 percent of the population by 2025, but they will make up only 8 percent of the population in developing countries (Bos, Vu, Levin, & Butalao, 1992). Even in small Pacific states, such as Niue, emigration of younger people means that the proportion of elderly residents has increased above the typical 4 percent or 5 percent distribution in developing countries (Barker, 1994). Increased longevity also is increasing the proportion in the category 75 years and older, predominantly women. It is anticipated that the population age ratio (75+/20–74) will continue to increase in developed countries from 0.0773 in 1990 to 0.1053 in 2020, and from 0.0251 to 0.0357 in developing countries over the same period (Keyfitz & Flieger, 1990).

Population aging is significant both in terms of absolute numbers of people and in the varying rates of change. As Neysmith (1991) noted, more than half the world's older people live in developing countries. Most of these are in Asia, including the world's two most populous countries, China and India. China's population in 1995 included 37.7 million men and 39.8 million women 65 years of age and older. In 2020, the numbers are expected to be 86.4 million for each sex. In India, there were 21.5 million men and 21.0 million women 65 years and older in 1995. This is expected to rise to 41.4 million and 43.6 million, respectively, in 2020 (Bos et al., 1992). These figures illustrate well the sheer numbers involved in population aging.

There are varying rates of increase of aging. Some countries, notably Japan, have rapidly experienced population aging. Japan faces large increases in the proportion of people who will be 80 years of age and older by 2025 (Korpi, 1995), as a result of both low fertility and the longest life expectancy in the world (Bos et al., 1992). Rapidly increased rates of aging are reported from the Caribbean (Brathwaite, 1989) and from sub-Saharan Africa, where the outcome has been aging in a context of poverty (Udvardy & Cattell, 1992). The effects have included conflict over the relationship between families and the state in Japan (Lechner & Sasaki, 1995) and problems of social isolation and economic vulnerability in other countries (Brathwaite, 1989; Udvardy & Cattell, 1992).

Demographers have posited the demographic transition theory to explain the aging of the world's populations as a result of the relationship between fertility and mortality, in which reduced fertility promotes population aging. Similarly, an epidemiological transition is used to explain lower mortality. Rowland (1991) argued that a gerontological transition occurs in which a momentum is created by young age structure and lower mortality—that is, increasing proportions of people will live longer and so develop an aging population profile. In the transition, there is a shift in the age structure from a pyramid shape to a rectangle, which reflects low population growth and low population momentum. In this gerontological transition the effects of different cohorts on patterns of aging can be examined and a picture of the diversity of aging can be produced. This is significant for the theorizing of a life course perspective on aging.

Perceptions of Demographic Change: Dependency, Care, and Resources

Global graying is sometimes identified as a problem because of perceptions about its negative effects, whether or not they are real. In general it is expected that graying will bring greater dependency as a result of greater longevity accompanied by chronic ill health. Warnes (1993) argued that the projected increase of older people in Europe to one-third of the population by 2050 is rather to be celebrated because it shows that people are living healthier lives, and with better education, housing, and income they should continue to contribute to society. According to Warnes, "In neither fiscal nor sociological terms is it proven or even likely that they will be an increasing burden on European society" (p. 99). Dependency accompanies frail health, but there is abundant evidence that the majority of older people live productive lives, with health expenses a significant cost only in the last years of life (Chawla & Kaiser, 1995; Kendig & McCallum, 1991).

Another concern is the anticipation that there will be an inadequate supply of caregivers because of smaller family sizes (for example, China's one-child policy and a resulting family structure of four grandparents, two parents, and one child), women's increasing participation in paid employment outside the home, and patterns of migration that result in increased emphasis on the nuclear family throughout the world. Evidence from various parts of the world indicates that care within the family is increasingly problematic (Tout, 1995), but generalization is difficult. In Japan, a strong cultural imperative remains for care within the family, and this is true of many other cultures (Chow, 1994; Lechner & Sasaki, 1995; Martin, 1991). In other places research shows a preference among older people for independent living. In the United States the phenomenon of elderly migration from one area to another is substantial, although it appears that migration after the age of 75 years is toward adult children (Clark & Wolf, 1992). Pampel (1992) noted the diversity of attitudes in Europe, and Korpi (1995) claimed that more older people in Sweden preferred to live alone.

It is also perceived that state finances will be inadequate to support the increasing dependency of older people. Vincent (1996) has drawn attention to the contradiction of arguing, as has been done in the United Kingdom, that there are too many old people in developed countries and at the same time arguing that there are too many young people in developing countries. This dilemma could be resolved by allowing open immigration of young people to developed countries, which would provide a larger working age group there. As controversial as this idea may be, it does show the difficulty of calculating dependency ratios and relying on them to guide policy. Predictions should consider changes in migration and labor market patterns. In Asia, for example, governments have a range of policies to reduce old-age dependency. These range from pronatalist policies in Singapore to immigration policies in Hong Kong, Singapore, Taiwan, and South Korea. They include changing pension rules and employment incentives in Japan (Martin, 1991) and mandating filial responsibility in China (Barusch, 1995).

Ideology and Structure

Perceptions of old age as a problem are mediated through values and the political–economic structure that produces specific relationships between the state and families. Both positive and negative values affect older people. Positive values are placed on family and a collective commitment to caring for others, but these positive values are confounded by negative ones. They include ageism, which defines older people as necessarily unproductive and dependent, and may be compounded by sexism and racism that discriminate against older women and older people from ethnic minorities. In addition, the definition of old age as primarily a medical problem is largely responsible for the fears about the costs of care of dependent older people in both developed and developing countries (Estes, 1991; Tout, 1995).

Aging also is affected by structural changes in the political economy. As Dominelli and Hoogvelt (1996) pointed out, globalization of the economy is a phenomenon with substantial effects on the welfare state. These effects are the result of the particular characteristics of global markets and their impact on production and national labor markets, and they include the privatization of welfare in developed countries and the use of developing countries as cheap sites for industrial development. Globalization is linked to the new economic rationalism (Rees & Rodley, 1995) that produces an emphasis on small government, privatization, and the new managerialism (Davies, 1995), as well as efficiency at the expense of effectiveness (Walker, 1993). It denies the social in favor of the economic.

The outcome of structural changes has included the restructuring of the labor market to the detriment of older workers, who face redundancy or early retirement with little chance of re-entering the labor market. In developed welfare states the existence of this cohort upsets the actuarial basis of social insurance schemes and exacerbates ageism because of fear of dependency (Guillemard & van Gunsteren, 1991). It is increasingly the negative view of aging that influences policy directions. In developing countries older people have been adversely affected by the shift from agricultural or pastoral economies and subsequent migration to cities (Levkoff, Macarthur, & Bucknall, 1995; McCallum, 1992).

The demographic increase in the older population is essentially conflated with value stereotypes and structural economic changes to produce a construction of old age as a social problem. This stereotype exists in spite of substantial evidence from around the world that older people can and do lead productive lives, including contributing financially and in child care to family support (Kendig & McCallum, 1991; Schulz, Borowski, & Crown, 1991). Whether age is a useful social category at all is debatable, given its diversity and the effects of structural change on how old age is defined (Guillemard & van Gunsteren, 1991; Tout, 1995). At question is the appropriate relationship among the state, the family, and the community and the autonomy of older people to live as citizens who share equal rights and duties. This relationship exists in an environment in which, increasingly, because of resource shortages, the distributive principle of need is stressed rather than principles, rights, and equality (Gibson, 1996; Shi, 1994; Walker, 1993).

STRUCTURAL CHANGE, FAMILY IMPACT, AND POLICY RESPONSES

Governments in developed societies have responded to all these challenges with policies for the labor market and social care that are generally considered inadequate. Old age is more and more defined by employment redundancy at ever-younger ages, and policies designed to retrain and reemploy older workers have been singularly unsuccessful (Laczko & Phillipson, 1991). In Australia, labor market restructuring has produced the need for a Mature Age Allowance social security benefit, which has replaced unemployment benefits for men ages 60 to 64. This change acknowledges the lack of jobs: For example, in New South Wales in 1994, long-term unemployment (52 weeks or more) affected nearly half of unemployed men and two-thirds of unemployed women in the 45 and older age group (George, 1996).

Most countries have moved toward community-based care to meet the needs of older people (Higgins, 1989). In many places there is increasing pressure on families to provide care. Filial support legislation exists in several countries, including some states in the United States. In China, it is mandated in the Marriage Laws of 1982 (Barusch, 1995), and the government of Singapore offers incentives for families caring for elderly parents (Teo, 1994). An additional trend in service provision is to contract out services, even though research evidence says this results in a decline in equity and access (Hugman, 1994a; Powell, 1996; Schmid, 1994). All these changes relate to economic efficiency without proper attention to family, community, and societal change.

Changes in the labor market in developed countries have led to greater unemployment among men in industrial jobs and increasing employment of women, particularly part-time employment. There is substantial evidence from Australia (Fine & Thomson, 1995), Japan, and the United States (Lechner & Sasaki, 1995) that the necessity of providing care means that women are leaving the work force, with a reduction in family income. Developing countries are also affected by labor market considerations. Structural adjustment policies have in some places resulted in inappropriate rural development, migration to urban centers, and family breakdown (Levkoff et al., 1995). As Chow (1994) noted, the dislocation of families means that old age in Asia is increasingly a problem of women, who are left in isolation through a combination of factors such as migration of younger family members, widowhood, and poverty occasioned by low income-earning ability. This situation is a subject of policy concern in the region (Economic and Social Commission for Asia and the Pacific/Japanese Organization for International Cooperation in Family Planning, 1991).

Current policy directions wrongly assume a homogeneity among older people and their families (Tout, 1989). Older people are themselves diverse in age, whether "young-old" or "old-old" chronologically. They differ in health status and in race, ethnicity, and sex distribution. Women, who experience greater longevity, make up the majority of old-age cohorts. Class also differentiates older people. In general, class divisions are deepened because of the differentiation of retirement income. In developed countries, private pensions and statutory programs differentiate classes of worker. In the developing world, where social security for older people is absent or minimal, gaps between rich and poor are maintained. It is important to note that financial support from children working in urban areas or abroad may mitigate old age poverty in developing countries.

Research from the Philippines (Watkins & Ulack, 1991) and Africa (Levkoff et al., 1995) indicates that, in developing countries, old people seem to be generally better off in rural rather than urban areas, where they can continue to work in an agricultural economy. This is true even though public services are less accessible (Chen & Jones, 1989). Of particular concern are the elderly refugees with multiple experiences of war and dislocation, for whom resettlement is most difficult (Levkoff et al., 1995; Vincent, 1995).

Changes in values are also important. Several studies in developing countries indicate that there are shifts in the traditional respect accorded older people, who in the past held high-status positions and were considered the source of wisdom, in some cases with mystical or magical powers (Udvardy & Cattell, 1992). Now elder abuse is an emerging problem. In developed countries, despite the evidence of strong family supports, there is evidence of a "growing dissociation between family kin networks and households, not just among the elderly, but also as a consequence of marital breakdown and household dissolution" (Hall, 1993, p. 101). Countries such as Canada, the United Kingdom, and Australia also have recently identified elder abuse as a serious problem.

There is also the question of resources. Resources from the public sector have been reduced in many places, if they existed at all, and families are increasingly expected to shoulder responsibility for their older members. This acceptance is traditionally expected in developing countries, and it is considered a matter of honor. However, the proper relationship between the state and families is a fundamental question in elder care. This question can be partially answered with respect to culture, but it must also be related to some foundation of moral principles. Thus, in developed countries there is a shift to community-based care without adequate resources. In both southern Europe and the developing countries, there is a propensity to reproduce institutional rather than community-based care, which parallels the development of high-technology urban hospitals—even though there is greater need for rural primary health care (Hugman, 1994a). In both cases, the appropriateness of care can be questioned.

SOCIAL WORK AND OLDER PEOPLE: RELEVANCE AND INTERVENTION

Both the diversity of global graying and the extraordinary global diversity of social work, with its varying range of educational arrangements, theoretical perspectives, organizational roles, and intervention strategies, make it difficult to examine the role of the social work profession in response to international aging. Social workers are intimately involved with social policy at all levels of practice, whether in grassroots individual and community work or management or policy planning, and the changes discussed in this chapter are relevant to practice at all these levels. What are the challenges facing social work in this arena of practice and policy, and how effective is social work in responding to these challenges?

Social work with older people is increasingly affected by such policy challenges as rationing of services and cost shifting from the state to families and from public to private agencies; these shifts restrict the ability of social workers to offer appropriate and adequate services. This cost shifting is manifest in the community care programs in many places where undue reliance is placed on family resources, leading to financial and psychological stress. As Levkoff and colleagues (1995) noted, rapid modernization leaves most developing countries without adequate services in place and an oversimplified view of natural or family-based care.

Reorientation of services through the new managerialism is another challenge. These new management strategies promote "de-skilling," where professional expertise is devalued, as Hugman (1994b) cogently argued with respect to the trend to care management, rather than case management. With the new managerialism the field of professional care in the public arena risks losing its caring values. Davies's (1995, p. 21) view of nursing, "good nursing is like invisible mending—much of it could not be seen" is equally applicable to social work, where so much of the work is hidden from people's view and is not easily amenable to these new management strategies.

An added concern is the social work role in situations in which the devaluing of older people is linked with ambivalence about the role of the state in providing services. As mediators between the state and families, social workers increasingly face inequities that deny social justice; for example, the recently announced nursing home access policy in Australia requires that people pay a substantial entry fee to obtain a nursing home place subsidized by the government. In another example—hip replacement surgery for frail older people—cost shifting leads to short hospital stay and rapid return to a nursing home. Few such nursing homes can offer rehabilitation that will lead to full mobility.

Social Work: Roles and Effectiveness

The effectiveness of social work is sometimes more a question of faith than of evidence, given the discrete and long-term nature of most social work interventions. That faith rests in the strengths that result from the social worker's role as a mediator between government policies and the effects of economic and social structures on individuals and their families. Social work operates at the margins of systems (Yelloly, 1995) and focuses on the social aspects of people's lives. Social work's strength, then, is its unique place among the helping professions: its focus on the social and its mediating role.

Social work specifically articulates values of social justice in its work at all levels of intervention. Of particular concern in work with older people are the values of autonomy, equity, and participation. Research shows that older people can be assisted in maintaining their autonomy even in institutional settings such as nursing homes, where rules, arrangements, and attitudes disempower residents. This parallels Goffman's phenomenon of the "total institution" (Gamroth, Semradek, & Tornquist, 1995; Lidz, Fischer, & Arnold, 1992). Without a concern for equity, social work could be coopted into bureaucratic priorities. Ensuring the participation of people in decisions affecting them is clearly a matter of social justice.

Social work's concern with social justice implies a commitment to social change and the improvement of people's well-being, and the profession is capable of drawing on a range of resources. Social work can work with change in the social, political, and economic context of practice, where its effectiveness depends on the way in which policy and practice are integrated. In the care of older people, this includes understanding the nature of welfare pluralism and the opportunities it may provide for innovative collaboration among state, nongovernment agencies, communities, and families (Evers, 1993).

Another potential strength is the scope of social work's strategies, which range from interpersonal to societal levels of intervention and embrace empowerment of individuals, families, and communities and advocacy with organizations on behalf of clients. In the field of aging, much is written about these strategies, and the effectiveness of social work is determined by the sophistication with which it implements them. For example, the concept of three-dimensional power identified by Lukes has been linked with people's biography and applied to empowerment strategies by Rees (1991). This approach is consonant with a social, as distinct from a psychological, orientation in social work. Evers (1993) has drawn attention to the need to understand old people's diversity, as well as political and economic forces, to construct appropriate and individualized services.

The literature on social work with older people draws attention to innovation and creative application of theories and techniques. An example is the use of the strengths perspective, which Saleeby (1996) described as moving from pathologizing to empowerment in a process of mutual growth for both social worker and client. The research literature shows vast numbers of innovative programs based on principles of empowerment and similar strategies, which are used in social work with individuals, families, and communities (Browne, 1995; Chapin, 1995; Dorfman, 1995; Evers & Svetlik, 1993; Korpi, 1995; Monaghan & Hooker, 1995; Motenko & Greenberg, 1995). Away from Europe and North America, community-based programs such as day centers are seen as empowering because older people can take an organizational role on the basis of good knowledge of their communities (Chow, 1994). These programs are adaptable to developed countries.

Social work's effectiveness in work with older people can be claimed, but it can also be questioned. Although many writers note the structural and ideological constraints on effective practice, less is said about practitioners' attitudes and values. Is it possible for social workers to avoid the ageism prevalent in society and organizational cultures? What commitment do social workers have to older people who generally face a future of worsening quality of life? For some, there is a clear commitment, but generally speaking, work with older people has been a neglected area in health and social services. This neglect, or distaste, may relate to the challenge such work presents to our own mortality and the model it presents of our futures and could exacerbate the style of professionalism, criticized by Orme (1996), which leads to patronizing community consultations by social work agencies. Orme argued for proper acknowledgment of older people's rights and participation in planning. A corollary of the de-skilling of professional social work through care management has been the relegation of geriatric social work to female practitioners with lesser skills (Hugman, 1994b).

Challenges for Social Work

There are no simple prescriptions for social work with older people as the 21st century approaches. Context has an immense effect on what can be achieved. A recent study of the effects of restructuring health services on the social work services in three Sydney, Australia, public teaching hospitals reveals substantial differences in professional work that reflect organizational structures and cultures (George & Napier, 1996). At a national level, the principles of resource allocation (national or local), service structures (institutional or community-based), and type of service provision (public, private nonprofit, or private for-profit) are variable. The world of the next century will be characterized by competition for resources and rapid policy changes, and it will require new skills and forms of practice. Social work's challenge is not only to improve its effectiveness but also to work with change. This will demand both practice and educational reform based in theory and a clear moral position.

Social work's challenge has several dimensions. First, old age must be reconceptualized in a way that avoids ageism, stigma, and patronage (Orme, 1996). The challenge is to see old age as a natural part of life rather than a problem. Recent theoretical approaches may help. The life course perspective seeks to identify the biography of people and acknowledge the diversity of their experiences as a prerequisite for appropriate services. It is time to question the conventional wisdom that older people should be helped to independence. If old age is seen as normal, then the inevitable dependency that comes with physical or mental frailty is also normal. Motenko and Greenberg (1995) said this reconceptualization would demand strategies that enabled self-awareness, but removed the guilt about failure to improve or being a burden to others, and promoted bonds of intergenerational reciprocity.

Second, social work is challenged to maintain clarity on its moral and ethical positions. Fundamentally, social workers are believed to share common values of equality, social justice, and principles of redistributive justice. Relativity is just not good enough when it comes to fundamental questions about human rights (Hugman, 1996). Doyal and Gough (1991) designated two essential universal needs, health and autonomy, as justifications for social intervention. The question of euthanasia is pertinent to the field of care of aged people and the debate includes the question of cultural relativism, which must be known and understood on a personal level.

The third challenge for social work is to accept change and work in new ways. One answer is the development of partnerships with other sectors, agencies, and professions (Braye & Preston-Shoot, 1993). The new managerialism is both a constraint and an opportunity that enables social work to improve its marginal position by forging alliances with nurses, doctors, informal caregivers, and the organizations of older people that act as government lobbying groups. Research has shown that older people are reluctant, for a variety of reasons, to lobby against elder abuse (Ginn, 1993; Harbison, 1996). This is just one area where a strategic and empowering alliance could improve the financing and provision of services.

The final challenge is to social work education. Old age is just one field of practice affected by similar macroeconomic and political trends that demand generic as well as specific social work knowledge and skills. Social workers of the future, wherever they practice, will need to be flexible and adaptable. They will need research skills to gain access to information; they will also need excellent skills in communication with diverse population groups. Social workers will also need to practice from clearly articulated values and be sophisticated about policy, both to understand the rapidly changing context of social work practice and to intervene strategically, with appropriate alliances, at the policy level.

An adult-centered learning approach is needed to develop these skills and capabilities. Such an approach draws on formal and prior experiential learning and promotes self-directedness, reflective practice, and lifelong learning (Candy, Crebert, & O'Leary, 1994; Margetson, 1994; Schön, 1987). There is increasing evidence of the effectiveness of innovative approaches based in these principles in social work education (Davis, George, & Napier, 1996; Taylor, 1996). As governments place increasing emphasis on narrowly defined and measurable competencies, it is essential for social work to restate its professional identity as an intellectual discipline and not merely a technical skill (Aldridge, 1996). This restatement is the ultimate challenge for the profession in the years ahead as social work responds to a changing context in which global graying is a major phenomenon.

Social Work's Response Through Social Development and Social Integration

The response of social work to these challenges is based on a belief in social development as a way forward that is applicable to both developing and developed countries (Midgley, 1995). The three dimensions of social development—poverty alleviation, productive employment, and social integration—are all pertinent to social work with older people. Many old people live in poverty in those many places where generous social insurance systems are not in place. Poverty accompanies the absence of productive employment when jobs disappear in labor market restructuring, and social integration is threatened by ageism and discrimination. It is incumbent on social work to include social development as part of its values, knowledge, and practice.

The most important and difficult challenge is to achieve social integration, with all it implies for participation, empowerment, autonomy, equality, and citizenship. In global graying, social integration is at risk in the face of divisive policies that promote the ageism that negatively affects families and communities. International social work must accept the challenge of integration of knowledge and skills in policy and practice and the promotion of social integration at the community and societal levels.

REFERENCES

Aldridge, M. (1996). Dragged to market: Being a profession in a postmodern world. *British Journal of Social Work, 26,* 177–194.

Barker, J. (1994). Home alone: The effect of out-migration on Niuean elders' living arrangements and social supports. *Pacific Studies, 17*(3), 41–81.

Barusch, A. (1995). Programming for family care of elderly dependents: Mandates, incentives and service rationing. *Social Work, 40,* 315–322.

Bos, E., Vu, M., Levin, A., & Butalao, R. (1992). *World population projections 1992–93 edition.* Baltimore: Johns Hopkins University Press.

Brathwaite, F. (1989). The elderly in the Commonwealth Caribbean: A review of research findings. *Ageing and Society, 9,* 297–304.

Braye, S., & Preston-Shoot, M. (1993). Empowerment and partnership in mental health: Towards a different relationship. *Journal of Social Work Practice, 7*(2), 115–128.

Browne, C. (1995). Empowerment in social work practice with older women. *Social Work, 40,* 358–364.

Candy, P., Crebert, G., & O'Leary, J. (1994). *Developing lifelong learners through undergraduate education.* Commissioned Report No. 28, National Board of Employment, Education and Training. Canberra, Australia: AGPS.

Chapin, R. (1995). Social policy development: The strengths perspective. *Social Work, 40,* 506–514.

Chen, A., & Jones, G. (1989). *Aging in ASEAN: Its socio-economic consequences.* Singapore: Institute of South East Asian Studies.

Chow, N. (1994). Elderly women in changing Asian societies. *Asia Pacific Journal of Social Work, 4*(2), 41–57.

Chawla, S., & Kaiser, M. (1995). The aged and development: Mutual beneficiaries. In Thursz, D., Nusberg, C., & Prather, J. (Eds.), *Empowering older people: An international approach* (pp. 151–182). Westport, CT: Auburn House.

Clark, R., & Wolf, D. (1992). Proximity of children and elderly migration. In A. Rogers (Ed.), *Elderly migration and population redistribution: A comparative study* (pp. 77–96). London: Belhaven Press.

Davies, C. (1995). Competence versus care? Gender and caring work revisited. *Acta Sociologica, 38,* 17–31.

Davis, A., George, J., & Napier, L. (1996). Hidden partners: Inviting change in the social work curriculum. *Proceedings, APASWE/ICSW Asia-Pacific/IFSW Regional Social Services Conference, Partnerships that work?* (pp. 93–97). Christchurch, New Zealand: University of Canterbury.

Dominelli, L., & Hoogvelt, A. (1996). Globalization and the technocratization of social work. *Critical Social Policy, 47*(16), 45–62.

Dorfman, R. (1995). Screening for depression among a well elderly population. *Social Work, 40,* 295–304.

Doyal, L., & Gough, I. (1991). *A theory of human need.* London: Macmillan.

Economic and Social Commission for Asia and the Pacific/Japanese Organization for International Cooperation in Family Planning, Inc. (1991). *Population aging in Asia.* New York: United Nations.

Estes, C. (1991). The new political economy of aging: Introduction and critique. In M. Minkler & C. Estes (Eds.), *Critical perspectives on aging: The political and moral economy of growing old* (pp. 19–36). New York: Baywood.

Evers, A. (1993). The welfare mix approach: Understanding the pluralism of welfare systems. In A. Evers & I. Svetlik (Eds.), *Balancing pluralism: New welfare mixes in care for the elderly* (pp. 3–32). Aldershot, England: Avebury.

Evers, A., & Svetlik, I. (Eds.). (1993). *Balancing pluralism: New welfare mixes in care for the elderly.* Aldershot, England: Avebury.

Fine, M., & Thomson, C. (1995). *Three years at home* (Social Policy Research Centre Reports and Proceedings, No. 121). Kensington, Australia: University of New South Wales.

Gamroth, L., Semradek, J., & Tornquist E. (1995). *Enhancing autonomy in long-term care.* New York: Springer.

George, J. (1996). The financial future of older Australians. *Proceedings, "Growing old in Australia" Forum* (pp. 28–33). Sydney: Medical Benefits Fund of Australia.

George, J., & Napier L. (1996). Conceptualising social work in health care. *Proceedings, IFSW/IASSW Joint Congress* (Vol. 3, pp. 227–229). Hong Kong: International Association of Schools of Social Work/International Federation of Social Workers/Hong Kong Social Work Association.

Gibson, D. (1996). Reforming aged care in Australia: Change and consequence. *Journal of Social Policy, 25*(2), 157–180.

Ginn, J. (1993). Gray power: Age-based organizations' response to structures inequalities. *Critical Social Policy, 13*(38), 23–47.

Guillemard, A.-M., & van Gunsteren, H. (1991). Pathways and their prospects: A comparative interpretation of the meaning of early exit. In M. Kohli, M. Rein, A.-M. Guillemard, & H. van Gunsteren (Eds.), *Time for retirement: Comparative studies of early exit from the labour force* (pp. 362–387). Cambridge, England: Cambridge University Press.

Hall, R. (1993). Family structures. In D. Noin & R. Woods (Eds.), *The changing population of Europe* (pp. 100–126). Oxford, England: Blackwell.

Harbison, J. (1996, May 2–3). *Responses to the mistreatment of older people: Ageism, policy and practice.* Paper presented at "Confronting Abuse: The Way Forward" Conference, Sydney.

Higgins, J. (1989). Defining community care: Realities and myths. *Social Policy and Administration, 23*(1), 3–16.

Hugman, R. (1994a). *Aging and the care of older people in Europe.* New York: St. Martin's Press.

Hugman, R. (1994b). Social work and case management in the U.K.: Models of professionalism and elderly people. *Ageing and Society, 14,* 235–254.

Hugman, R. (1996). Social work ethics: Conflict or compromise? *Proceedings, IFSW/IASSW Joint Congress* (pp. 140–142). Hong Kong: International Association of Schools of Social Work/International Federation of Social Workers/Hong Kong Social Work Association.

Kendig, H., & McCallum, J. (Eds.). (1991). *Grey policy: Australian policies for an ageing society.* Sydney, Australia: Allen & Unwin.

Keyfitz, N., & Flieger, W. (1990). *World population growth and aging: Demographic trends in the late twentieth century.* Chicago: University of Chicago Press.

Korpi, W. (1995). The position of the elderly in the welfare state: Comparative perspectives in old-age care in Sweden. *Social Service Review,* 242–273.

Laczko, F., & Phillipson, C. (1991). *Changing work and retirement.* Milton Keynes, England: Open University Press.

Lechner, V., & Sasaki, M. (1995). Japan and the United States struggle with who will care for our aging parents when caregivers are employed. *Journal of Gerontological Social Work, 24*(1/2), 97–114.

Levkoff, S., Macarthur, I., & Bucknall, J. (1995). Elderly mental health in the developing world. *Social Science and Medicine, 41,* 983–1003.

Lidz, C., Fischer, L., & Arnold, R. (1992). *The erosion of autonomy in long-term care.* New York: Oxford University Press.

Margetson, D. (1994). Current educational reform and the significance of problem-based learning. *Studies in Higher Education, 19*(1), 5–19.

Martin, L. (1991). Population aging policies in East Asia and the United States. *Science, 251,* 527–531.

McCallum, J. (1992). Asia Pacific retirement: Models for Australia, Fiji, Malaysia, Philippines and Republic of Korea. *Journal of Cross-Cultural Gerontology, 7,* 25–43.

Midgley, J. (1995). *Social development: The developmental perspective in social welfare.* Thousand Oaks, CA: Sage Publications.

Monaghan, D., & Hooker, K. (1995). Health of spouse caregivers of dementia patients: The role of personality and social support. *Social Work, 40*, 305–314.

Motenko, A., & Greenberg, S. (1995). Reframing dependence in old age: A positive transition for families. *Social Work, 40*, 382–390.

Neysmith, S. (1991). Dependency among Third World elderly: A need for new direction in the nineties. In M. Minkler & C. Estes (Eds.), *Critical perspectives on aging: The political and moral economy of growing old* (pp. 311–321). New York: Baywood.

Orme, J. (1996). Participation or patronage: Changes in social work practice brought about by community care policies in Britain. *Proceedings, IFSW/IASSW Joint Congress* (pp. 250–252). Hong Kong: International Association of Schools of Social Work/International Federation of Social Workers/Hong Kong Social Work Association.

Pampel, F. (1992). Trends in living alone among the elderly in Europe. In A. Rogers (Ed.), *Elderly migration and population redistribution* (pp. 97–117). London: Belhaven Press.

Powell, M. (1996). Granny's footsteps, fractures and the principles of the NHS. *Critical Social Policy, 47*(16) 27–44.

Rees, S. (1991). *Achieving power: Practice and policy in social welfare.* Sydney, Australia: Allen & Unwin.

Rees, S., & Rodley, G. (Eds.). (1995). *The human costs of managerialism: Advocating the recovery of humanity.* Sydney, Australia: Pluto Press.

Rosenman, L., Le Broque, R., & Carr, S. (1994). The impact of caring upon the health of older women. *Australian Journal of Public Health, 18*(4), 440–444.

Rowland, D. (1991). *Ageing in Australia.* Melbourne, Australia: Longman Cheshire.

Saleeby, D. (1996). The strengths perspective in social work practice: Extensions and cautions. *Social Work, 41*(3), 296–305.

Schmid, H. (1994). Government's changing policy in the provision of home care services for Israel's frail elderly. *International Journal of Sociology and Social Policy, 14*(3–5), 38–53.

Schön, D. (1987). *Educating the reflective practitioner.* London: Jossey-Bass.

Shi, L. (1994). Elderly support in rural and suburban villages: Implications for future support system in China. *Social Science and Medicine, 39*, 265–277.

Schulz, J., Borowski, A., & Crown, W. (1991). *Economics of population aging: The "graying" of Australia, Japan and the United States.* New York: Auburn House.

Taylor, I. (1996). Enquiry and action learning: Empowerment in social work education. In M. Preston-Shoot & S. Jackson (Eds.), *Educating social workers in a changing policy context.* (pp. 171–189). London: Whiting & Birch.

Teo, P. (1994). The national policy on elderly people in Singapore. *Ageing and Society, 14*, 405–427.

Tout, K. (1989). *Aging in developing countries.* Oxford, England: Oxford University Press.

Tout, K. (1995). The aging perspective on empowerment. In D. Thursz, C. Nusberg, & J. Prather (Eds.), *Empowering older people: An international perspective* (pp. 3–36). Westport, CT: Auburn House.

Udvardy, M., & Cattell, M. (1992). Gender, aging and power in sub-Saharan Africa: Challenges and puzzles. *Journal of Cross-Cultural Gerontology, 7,* 275–288.

Vincent, J. (1995). *Inequality and old age.* London: UCL Press.

Vincent, J. (1996). Who's afraid of an aging population? *Critical Social Policy, 47*(16), 3–26.

Walker, A. (1993). Under new management: The changing role of the state in the care of older people in the United Kingdom. *Journal of Aging and Social Policy, 5*(1–2), 127–154.

Warnes, A. (1993). Demographic ageing: Trends and policy responses. In D. Noin, & R. Woods (Eds.), *The changing population of Europe* (pp. 82–99). Oxford, England: Blackwell.

Watkins, J., & Ulack, R. (1991). Migration and regional population again in the Philippines. *Journal of Cross-Cultural Gerontology, 6,* 383–411.

World Bank. (1993). *World development report 1993.* New York: Oxford University Press.

Yelloly, M. (1995). Professional competence and higher education. In M. Yelloly & M. Henkel (Eds.), *Learning and teaching in social work.* London: Jessica Kingsley.

6

International Social Development and Social Work

A Feminist Perspective

LENA DOMINELLI

As the end of the 20th century approaches, academic discourse on social development continues to accord low priority to examining either women's role in the developmental process or its specific impact on women's well-being. Despite Boserup's (1970) long-standing seminal work in identifying the absence of women, their contributions and their concerns in international initiatives, women continue to be at best "added on" to policy documents, including the recent publications on social development that have followed the United Nations Summit for Social Development in Copenhagen in March 1995. Besides "adding" women's concerns to their agenda, these writings treat women as a largely unified and homogeneous category. This approach is unfortunate. It misses both the specificity and the complexity of women's lives, and in doing so ignores their realities as they experience them. Hence, policies emanating from an official vantage point are inadequate because they only partly address women's specific interests as women; and they do not take account of women's relevant cultural, spiritual, and ethnic sensitivities.

This gap must be remedied by fully incorporating women in their diversity into the social development process on women's own terms. Meeting this goal requires locality-specific interventions designed and controlled by the women of the area themselves. External expertise is necessary primarily for those items of knowledge and skills that are not held by local women. Even then, however, external experts can be of greater assistance if they work under the jurisdiction of the local women and are accountable to them. The accessibility of financial resources and the conditions under which these become available to grassroots activists must include similar principles if their relevance to local women's needs is to be maximized. A feminist perspective that can respond to the specificities of the situation and draw on the commonalities these highlight vis-à-vis other women is invaluable in meeting the objective of providing women-driven and gender-sensitive responses to social development (Jayawardena, 1995).

In this chapter, a feminist perspective is used to examine social development, its impact on women, and its capacity to implement women-driven agendas and find ways that can heighten social development's responsiveness to women across a range of social divisions and regions. The implications of such an approach for the development of feminist social work theory and practice are also discussed.

SOCIAL DEVELOPMENT

Social development has been counterpoised with economic development to signify a focus on civil society and its diverse organizations at the level of community (Gray, Mazibuko, & O'Brien, 1996; Midgley 1995), yet these two dimensions of social life are interrelated and interdependent. Moreover, they are gendered and stratified according to myriad other social divisions. However, the dominant ideology expounded in the development literature is that women's activities are usually rooted in community functions that revolve around the reproduction of families on both a daily and a generational basis, while men dominate the public sphere of economic transactions (Chowdhry, 1995; Mohanty, 1995). To counteract such vague generalizations about women's economic and social activities, there is a need for detailed descriptions and analyses covering the specifics, whereby these tasks are carried out and the details of how these vary according to locale. These studies will be of subsequent use in informing the development process.

Social development consists of interventions aimed at providing the conditions whereby human beings change existing social relations by using resources to express their creativity and grow to their full potential. Insofar as an individual cannot achieve this aim on his or her own, the processes used in reaching this goal involve others. They are social rather than merely personal and draw on power dynamics for their realization. A crucial issue is how and on what terms one person contributes to the social fulfillment of others. If the basis on which this development proceeds affirms relations of domination, then exploitation and oppression result.

In other words, there is nothing in social development itself that makes it ipso facto either a liberationist or emancipatory process. It is for this reason that having perspectives that take account of the power relations inherent within any given social development process is so important. A feminist perspective that focuses on social divisions and the resulting power relations can assist in the understanding and exposure of the power dynamics embedded in social development projects.

However, merely holding a feminist perspective guarantees neither an accurate rendition of women's role in social development nor an appropriate form of involvement with social development projects from women's point of view. Marchand and Parpart (1995) provided a trenchant critique of the failure of feminists, particularly white middle-class ones residing in the West, writing about women in what has been called the "Third World,"[1] to deconstruct the category "woman" in much of the development literature they have crafted. Although these feminists' input has resulted in the inclusion of women's concerns in the social development agenda, this has been done chiefly on an ad hoc basis and has not led to social changes to promote the interests of women. An analysis of their texts reveals that some feminist authors have increased the burdens carried by women in industrializing countries by treating them as a homogeneous group whose achievements lag behind those of their white Western sisters (Marchand & Parpart, 1995). Their writings have produced these results by denying "Third World" women their agency—that is, their capacity to act on their own behalf as they see fit, and have robbed them of their rights to self-determination (Chowdhry, 1995). These women are presented as victims of globalizing economic forces that dictate and determine their behavior at the level of community (Mohanty, 1995). Portraying women in this way is often racist because it affords privilege to white Western women's accomplishments, sometimes even at the expense of disparaging those of black women (or women of color) in the West (Bald, 1995; Raissiguier, 1995). It is essential to take account of women's capacity to individually and collectively adapt to circumstances and affect the external factors that shape their own lives and those of their families. This recognition ensures that women's achievements are recorded and acknowledged in ways that reflect women's agency and determination to assert their own dreams and aspirations on seemingly omnipotent impersonal forces.

[1] "Third World" is in quotes to denote the problematic nature of the term. Here it refers to women who live outside Western countries, without implying either homogeneity or inferiority.

It is important to highlight the role that linguistic conventions play in human communications. Language is problematic because words have embedded within them certain power relations that are taken for granted (Spender, 1970). The issue becomes relevant because the categories "women of color" and "black women" run the risk of essentializing certain groups of women in particular ways and treating them as if they were a homogeneous category. The term "black women" denotes that the women referred to have had their life choices shaped by the existence of racism and undermined by it. A political use of this term acknowledges the social construction of racism and offers a signification that a group or groups of women are at the receiving end of racist dynamics perpetrated by others. This does not imply that all these women are the same, or that their experiences of racism are identical. The term "black women" is preferable to "women of color," a term common in North America, because this alternative wording is equally problematic. It holds the suggestion that "white" women are the "normal" or dominant color, which does not have to be identified as such.[2]

FEMINIST ANALYSES

Feminists the world over have played a major role in highlighting the importance of gender in the development process. However, this has not always been done in a manner that reflects a sensitivity to power differentials derived from the various social divisions that exist among women. As a result, women in diverse parts of the world have been erroneously treated as a homogeneous category sharing identical interests and concerns. Problematic as this has been, the issue has been compounded by the special privilege given to the viewpoint of Western feminists, who have spoken from a position of assumed superiority about other women with whom they have little in common. Consequently, there has been an "othering" of poor women in many parts of the globe by richer women who have appropriated the voice and rights of these women to shape their own destiny (hooks, 1994). The women who have been "othered" have not passively ignored this violation of their integrity. They have responded assertively to put straight the record of their achievements and in the process have contributed to the further development of feminist theory and practice (Amos

[2] It should be noted that Irish women and Jewish women in Britain experience their own particular forms of racism, even though their skin is white.

& Parmar, 1984; Carby, 1982; Chowdhry, 1995). In the West, for example, "black women's" critiques have encouraged self-reflection among white feminists, who have consequently become more sensitive to issues of racism in their own writings (Dominelli, 1992; hooks, 1994).

The assumption that gender oppression causes women to share similar concerns and problems was made in the early days of the second wave of feminism, primarily by white middle-class women activists in the United States (Friedan, 1963; Morgan, 1970). Their focus on white middle-class women's lack of fulfillment in the social arena, inadequate relationships with doctors who controlled their health and reproductive rights, and restricted sexual expression gave a particular direction to their movement (Frankfort, 1972). However, its white middle-class bias was ignored by both these feminists and the mass media, which presented their issues as if all women faced them in the same way. The widespread publicity that followed their actions defined feminism as the activities of young, white, able-bodied, middle-class women. This meant that the voices of many other women in the United States—white working-class, black middle-class, black working-class, older, and disabled women, among others—were discounted.

Reality was more complex. It was not so much that these issues were irrelevant to other women. Rather, their priorities, even in these general areas, lay elsewhere. For example, white middle-class American women had access to health care, and poor, white and black working-class women did not. Moreover, while white, middle-class women were being encouraged to have more children, poor black women were being sterilized against their wishes (Sidel, 1987). In other parts of the world, poor women's priorities have often centered on matters of basic survival: food for their children to eat, clean water to drink, fuel, housing, remunerated work, education, and primary health care. These differing material realities have influenced women's decisions about where to expend their energies.

In addition, poor women were themselves taking active steps to improve their conditions (Mohanty, 1995). They were not waiting passively for middle-class Western women to tell them what to do, yet feminist works describing their activities have often assumed and highlighted their status as victims of either capitalist forces, including the World Bank and the International Monetary Fund, or the private patriarchy practiced by men in their own countries (Mohanty, 1995). In other words, women who were different from those doing the writing were denied agency and treated as charitable cases who required intervention for their salvation by their more liberated counterparts in the West. Marchand and Parpart

(1995) argued that these dynamics reinforced neocolonial relations among women.

White middle-class feminists in the West have sought to respond to these critiques of their work (hooks, 1994). For example, to convey the message that different strategies and options are required by different groups of women, British and American feminists have altered their struggles around abortion to emphasize "women's reproductive rights" rather than advocating "abortion on demand" (Dominelli, 1988; Dominelli & McLeod, 1989). In industrializing countries, the feminist agenda articulated through Development Alternatives for Women for a New Era (DAWN) represented a move toward the fuller acknowledgment of women's specific needs in development projects (Sen & Grown, 1987).

This strategy has not been completely successful. The issues that continue to gain media attention in industrialized countries have tended to be those advocated by white, middle-class women, even with regard to the issues given prominence by poor women in industrializing countries. This state of affairs partly reflects the fact that white, middle-class women in the West have the time to articulate their agenda, the means to convey it to a larger audience, and a readier access to the mass media worldwide. On the theoretical terrain and further afield, the key architects of the DAWN program, Sen and Grown (1987), have been criticized for treating the division of labor as the defining characteristic that universalizes women's experiences. Mohanty (1991) suggested that the division of labor women actually implement varies according to locality and time, a position that should be evident in feminist analyses. Without this, Mohanty (1991) maintained that the level of abstraction encompassed by the term "the division of labor," as used by Sen and Grown (1987), subsumes the specificities of women's diverse experiences. Thus, it homogenizes women's practices and creates a false sense of commonality around the various oppressions that women encounter in their working environments.

These criticisms are valid. Feminists need to address them if feminism is to become inclusive of the initiatives of all women throughout the world who seek to improve the conditions under which they live. In finding ways of dealing with and valuing differences across a range of social divisions, feminists can ensure that women's diversity and agency are respected in both theory and practice. However, care must be exercised to ensure that identity politics are not pursued merely for their own sake because this will not produce the theoretical advances feminists need to bridge the enormous divisions that exist among women. This danger arises because focusing only on difference leads to reductionism that isolates women as individuals within a given nexus and precludes the possibility of women acting in solidarity around particular issues as they define them.

For collective forms of organizing to be enacted, women have to find ways of theorizing that value and respect differences and simultaneously address the power imbalances among them. This process is likely to produce a diversity of contributions because the processes involved in bringing women together should be those that enable each woman to contribute from her own strengths and vantage point. Such a way of working also helps each woman augment the efforts of others, rather than competing with them. This methodology has been illustrated by the Greenham Common Women's Peace Movement, for example (Cook & Kirk, 1983; Dominelli, 1986). Women must actively seek out common ground if initiatives that benefit a particular group are to be supported by large numbers of other women.

A commonality of interests cannot be assumed: Doing so ignores women's own roles in reproducing oppressive relationships. Women need to acknowledge that they can be and have been involved in oppressing other women—for example, white, middle-class women's oppression of black women employed as domestic workers (Collins, 1990). The dynamics whereby oppressive situations arise among women have to be and understood so that those women who currently oppress others can learn to act in nonoppressive ways. Doing so requires women to be open, self-critical, and capable of envisaging multiple aspects to their identities. They must understand that this multiplicity enables them to oppress others and, at the same time, be oppressed themselves. For example, white, middle-class women in the West have been complicit in reinforcing racist practices and benefiting from racist relations, although they were simultaneously being oppressed by their own menfolk. Thus, sisterhood cannot be taken for granted. Common interests must be identified through analyses that focus on specific contexts and activities. Following through on such processes becomes even more important in an international context. Moreover, relations of sisterhood will not happen without women committing themselves individually and collectively to relating to other women in egalitarian ways and then taking specific steps to ensure that these are realized.

Feminism is well placed to assist women in pursuing this project. It has the philosophical underpinnings, analytical tools, and forms of practice that enable women to work in a nonoppressive manner if they are committed to such ways of working. Its capacity to guide women toward critical self-appraisal, reflexivity, listening to what other women have to say, and integrating theory and practice is crucial. Feminism should not be considered a method that magically enables women to act in egalitarian ways, however. Women are the product of the divided societies in which they live (Dominelli & McLeod, 1989), and they, too, are imperfect beings who have to consciously work for egalitarian relations in their interactions with other women, with children, and with men.

FEMINISM, SOCIAL DEVELOPMENT, AND SOCIAL WORK

Social work is responsible for enhancing people's well-being and purports to change individuals so that they can enhance their potential to take control of their lives (Dominelli & McLeod, 1989). Many of its concerns and activities overlap with those of interest to professionals advocating social development. In some instances, social development is considered one of the many forms social work assumes (Gray, Mazibuko, & O'Brien, 1996). At other times, social workers and workers on social development projects are employed by different authorities but work collaboratively (Kaseke, 1994).

Social work as a discipline can be parochial in its outlook, focusing largely on a specific situation from a given cultural perspective. In some countries—for example, the United States—this parochial perspective has focused the competence of social work primarily on therapeutic interventions, which exclude a perception of the broader social forces that affect people's behavior (Davis, 1994). On the other hand, an emphasis on social development is prominent in many of the industrializing countries (Midgley, 1995). This approach enables social workers to transcend the limitations of exclusively therapeutic interventions.

In becoming more social development–oriented and international in outlook, social work needs to ensure that it does not become another means of reproducing neocolonial relations and neglect the needs of the individual within the social context. Social work's record on this front is not strong. In many countries, its preoccupation with controlling individuals and groups or rationing state monies has contributed to disenfranchising claimants from social resources and exacerbated their disadvantaged economic position. Moreover, social workers in a number of countries have historically been deeply implicated in denying certain groups of people agency in determining their own destiny. For example, aboriginal peoples in North America, Australia, and New Zealand have been deprived of their cultural heritage by the residential schools for their children (Armitage,

1995; Behrendt, 1996; Haig-Brown, 1988). Nonetheless, the role of social work in society, and its relationship to social development in emancipatory terms, are issues that must be specifically addressed.

Social work has sometimes contributed to the reinforcement of oppressive relations by being indifferent to the notion of empowerment, often naively believing that its commitment to "doing what is in people's best interests" was good enough. For example, gender oppression has not always been a crucial concern of social workers. There has been an assumption that because most social workers and their clients are women, sexism is not an issue for the profession (Dominelli, 1991a). White social workers have failed to respond adequately to the charge of racial oppression embedded within their own practice (Ahmad, 1990; Devore & Schlesinger, 1986; Dominelli, 1988). Similar issues arise with regard to the oppression of working-class clients by middle-class social workers (Bolger, Corrigan, Davis, & Frost, 1981; Corrigan & Leonard, 1978). The disability movement has also protested social workers' failure to respond to the specific needs of disabled people and proposed alternative ways of relating to them (Morris, 1992; Oliver, 1990), as have older women (Mazuki 1992), lesbians (Hanscombe & Forrest, 1982), and gay men (Plummer, 1981), among others.

Although issues of oppression through social work practice and the welfare system have assumed greater prominence since the early 1970s, the profession in general has a long way to go in developing antioppressive practice. Even those social workers who espouse the validity of such a concern for the profession have difficulty with its implementation. Thus, despite feminists' commitment to and search for emancipatory forms of practice and the key roles that they have played in identifying the debilitating impact oppression has had on people's lives, feminist social workers have sometimes contributed to furthering the processes of exclusion emanating from various types of oppression. For example, Wilson (1996) presented a moving portrait of how feminist practitioners in a women's refuge in Australia have perpetrated racist practices right up to the present day, notwithstanding their intentions to the contrary. However, this need not be the case, as Jayawardena (1995) demonstrated in her powerful account of Western feminists' contribution to social development processes in India during British rule.

Social workers do not have to act in accordance with oppressive social relations that reinforce psychological violence and predations in social work. They can pursue a viable option by changing their practice to support social change that will liberate people, although they do need to consider the risks in this approach. Their vulnerability as social workers may increase if they choose to work in ways that challenge existing inegalitarian social relations. However, a greater susceptibility to risk need not preclude social workers from acting in ways that promote the well-being of clients. They can take calculated risks knowing what the consequences of their choice might be. Furthermore, acting in a manner that is consistent with the ethics and ideals of the profession makes assisting people's struggles to be free consistent with social workers' professional behavior.

Raising the international profile of the profession can be difficult for locality-trained social workers. Given that each can speak only from her or his own specific knowledge base and experience, she or he may come across as colonizing, despite a commitment to egalitarianism. When this problem is identified, social workers must not become defensive, but apologize, learn from their mistakes, and seek to do better in the future. If they can accept that their forays into the international arena are tentative, imbued with humility and a desire to understand the other person's point of view in the pursuit of social justice for all, social workers can begin to engage in a mutual dialogue to develop the theories and tools that will equip social work as a profession to carry this project forward.

A number of social problems encountered by social workers worldwide give them the opportunity to intervene in emancipatory ways. These include poverty, family breakdown, violence against women and children, child abuse and neglect, isolated elderly people, and criminal behavior. Help for these problems is basic to social development. They are evident in all countries, although the forms they take, the specific people affected, the types of interventions carried out, and the legal framework within which social workers operate vary from nation to nation. How can social workers operate in these matters in a locality-specific mode and also theorize and practice in ways that would identify and develop nonoppressive international connections?

The International Association of Schools of Social Work (IASSW) sought to respond to this question by taking the issue of violence against women as its theme for the United Nations' Fourth World Conference on Women in Beijing in September 1995. This response was organized by a group of feminist social work academics who were members of IASSW's Women's Caucus. It was innovative work and marked a first for those who sought to represent social work educators in an international forum of this nature. The problem of unity within diversity was addressed by having different countries present their own work and concerns under this umbrella and then produce a set of agreed guidelines for action that were broad enough to enable social workers in different countries to interpret and implement them as they saw fit. It is still too early to evaluate the success or failure of this approach, but it does provide an example of a complex social problem that is dispersed throughout the globe being tackled by women who share a commitment to working with each other in nonoppressive ways.

Despite the usefulness of this initiative in highlighting the importance of egalitarian processes, it has not yet adequately addressed the need to develop a feminist analytical framework. Such a framework should incorporate the idea of unity within diversity as part of a feminist practice that carries the confidence of a global network of social workers and their clients. Social workers should not be daunted by the prospect of addressing this issue. An impressive array of feminist writings by both white and black women can assist social work academics and practitioners in this task.

To a considerable extent, social work has already been influenced by feminist theory and practice (Dominelli, 1992, 1997). There is a body of feminist literature that can be drawn on to create more gender-sensitive and locally specific forms of intervention, including work by Ahmad (1990), Bhavani (1993), Bozalek (1996), Burden and Gottlieb (1987), Collins (1990), Dave and Desai (1996), Dominelli (1990, 1991b), Dominelli and McLeod (1989), Hanmer and Statham (1987), Jayawardena (1995), Langan and Day (1992), Marchant and Wearing (1986), Meng (1996), and Wilson (1996).

These works offer a number of tenets that social workers can usefully incorporate into their practice as they seek to develop a form of social development recognizing that a number of localized social problems occur across the globe and may have some elements, including possible causes, in common. These include

- integrating theory and practice.
- facilitating the expression of women's own voices.
- listening to women.
- working in partnership with women.
- turning private woes into public issues.
- seeking collective solutions to social problems.
- acknowledging the interdependence that exists among members of any given locality or community, including the international one.
- recognizing the interplay between women's unpaid work in the home and in the paid labor market.

- acknowledging the interaction between women's responsibility to care for others and to looking after their own needs as women.
- validating and valuing women's experiences, skills, and knowledge.
- according individual women dignity and respect in any contact with them.
- following principles and methods that enhance the welfare of children, men, and women.

This list is not exhaustive and there is some overlap among its various postulates. The integration of theory and practice refers to the attempt to ensure that there is consistency between feminist thought and the actions that feminists undertake in practice when working with women. This includes a unity between the ends feminists pursue and the means used in reaching them. Thus, unlike orthodox Marxists who have argued that all will be well come the revolution, feminists seek to ensure that developments in the field today reflect their aspirations for tomorrow (Dominelli & McLeod, 1989).

Listening to women's own voices is used to signify the importance that feminists attach to the view that one woman or group of women should not speak for other women (Burden & Gottlieb, 1987; Collins, 1990). Following through on this axiom acknowledges the diversities women represent. In addition, this guideline is aimed at counteracting the invisibility of women's contributions to society and the silencing of their views on social events of import that have traditionally marked women's place in the world as an inferior one (Hanmer & Statham, 1987). It also draws on the principle of valuing women's experiences, skills, and knowledge (Hanmer & Statham, 1987; Langan & Day, 1990).

This mode of working does not mean that women cannot be critical of each other's contributions and perspectives. Indeed, self-reflection and the ability to respond to critiques that women have made about other women's positions has been a source of dynamism and growth in feminist theory and practice (Dominelli & McLeod, 1989; hooks, 1994). It does not mean that feminist practitioners need to create the spaces in which women can speak for themselves and set their own agenda for action (Cook & Kirk, 1983). Sensitive self-criticism is constructive and indicates how women can demonstrate respect for each other. Mutual respect is a crucial factor in women being able to treat each other with dignity. Moreover, in taking what women have to say for themselves seriously, feminists are also playing a role in validating the experiences and skills of women who disagree with or differ from themselves. When they respond to others in this way, feminists are also demonstrating that they are actively listening to women (Burden & Gottlieb, 1987). Social workers who can do this are better able to establish a partnership between themselves as workers and the women with whom they work. Working with them along these lines in turn enables professionals to develop more egalitarian relations with the women and, subsequently, to free women's own capabilities for taking control of their lives and making decisions about what they with to do with themselves.

Working together in a more egalitarian manner allows women to explore their seemingly individualized problems, move on to uncover the social basis on which their lives are predicated, ascertain the constraints inherent in their situations, evaluate their potentials for growth, and seek collective solutions to the social problems they encounter. The ability to highlight connections among women and expose similarities in their positions is an important skill for feminist practitioners to deploy.

It also helps to counter the feelings of isolation and fragmentation that shapes the experience of many women in their day-to-day routines. Bringing out the commonalities that underpin much of women's daily experiences, despite the different social positions they may occupy, is crucial in turning private woes into social issues (Burden & Gottlieb, 1980; Dominelli & McLeod, 1989). Women's abilities to behave in this way have attracted wide publicity and a broad spectrum of support; for example, campaigns against domestic violence in Australia, Britain, Canada, India, and the United States.

Such activities underpin the way in which feminist networks operate and are crucial in revealing the interdependence that exists between any group of women and the issue they seek to address. It also highlights how different aspects of women's lives fit together and emphasizes the holistic approach endorsed by feminist social work practice (Dominelli & McLeod, 1989). Feminist social actions and campaigns against domestic violence demonstrate how feminists may need to challenge existing definitions about social phenomena and redefine them in ways that lend weight to their concerns. In cases of domestic violence, feminists have questioned the way in which private life and public life have been demarcated and have shown how traditional definitions can obscure the exploitation and maltreatment of women and children (Dominelli & McLeod, 1989; Hanmer & Statham, 1987; Langan & Day, 1990). Similar points have been made about sexual violence in the family (Rush, 1980). Paid and unpaid work is another area in which feminist social action has highlighted the interdependence that exists between different aspects of women's lives.

Feminists have identified how women's responsibilities in unpaid caring for others in the privacy of the home shape their positions in the wage-earning labor market (Walby, 1990).

Moreover, as feminists have unraveled the complexities of women's lives and shown the interdependence that exists among women, children, and men, they have pointed out avenues by which the lives of women, children, and men can be enhanced. Thus, women's unwillingness to have men excluded from child care responsibilities and refusal to condone men's violence against others have been critical in promoting a better quality of life for all people (Bowl, 1985; Connell, 1995). Although women are the starting point of feminist action, the repercussions of feminism go well beyond that. Feminism has been important in demonstrating that men have gendered identities, too, and in rejecting the false universalism of men's experience, despite its traditional portrayal as such in both common parlance and scientific discourse.

These principles are not unfamiliar to social workers—they are paralleled in social work's existing professional ethics and value base. Thus, they can provide the foundation for practitioners to move from a known and understood territory to an unknown one when they are seeking to help women achieve their self-defined goals of self-sufficiency and independence. However, for social workers to be able to work in women-centered ways that endorse women's determination to live in a nonoppressive environment, they must be prepared to intervene as professionals who put their expertise at the service of the women concerned, rather than relating to them as distanced authority. Placing themselves at the disposal of the women concerned is a reversal of the traditional tenets of professionalism (Hugman, 1991). Changing the client–social worker relationship in this way also frees practitioners to respond supportively to women who wish to challenge current social arrangements and shift them in more progressive directions. In supporting these women, social workers are endorsing feminism's commitment to eradicating oppressive social relations.

The commitment to social change in improving women's plight marks feminism's departure from a more traditional woman-centered approach to social work practice. Although these two approaches have several features in common, there are major differences. Traditional women-centered proposals can be confined to endorsing a status quo that may continue to oppress women by drawing them more closely into its ambit. A community care policy that relies on women to provide unpaid care to needy individuals, in addition to the paid and unpaid work they already do and is used to reduce public expenditure on care work, is an example of a woman-centered policy. Such a policy adds to the exploitation of women as workers whose contribution to the social good is assumed and thereby socially devalued and marginalized in consequence. At the end of the day, women's only weapon against oppression may be their ability to say no to further exploitation. Social workers have a responsibility to endorse women's stand in such circumstances, if they are working with them in ways that are consistent with empowerment approaches or have a feminist orientation. In following feminist precepts, social workers are creating spaces in which people can tell and act out their own stories instead of following those that are externally imposed. They are also enabling people to articulate the connections they experience between structural oppression and personal suffering.

Social workers practicing in local communities can collect detailed information about the ways in which women live their daily lives, how they cope with their families' traumas and crises, and how they develop strategies of survival for themselves and their families that indicate determination and strength in the face of immense odds such as poverty, violence, and loneliness. Social workers can go public with such information, drawing on their access to various communities and their interventions in them as investigative tools and sources of reliable data collection. These can be used to challenge official research that tries to gloss over the harsh realities that poor people, the majority of whom are women and children, endure on a daily basis. In this way, social work practice becomes a way of doing research and encourages the development of a reflective practitioner in the manner advocated by Schön (1983). This methodology can be used by both male and female social workers, and it has relevance and applicability to children, men, and women. It also becomes a way of centering people who are accustomed to being marginalized and having their needs and voices neglected by officialdom. In short, it provides a model paradigm for social work as social development.

CONCLUSION

As the world moves toward the 21st century, there has been a rise of fundamentalist religious movements and political ideologies that seek to turn back the social gains women have recently achieved in both the East and the West. Although these developments have made women's struggles for liberation seem more precarious now than at any other point since the 1960s, the picture is not altogether gloomy. Women are organizing on their own behalf in every part of the world. Social workers can become involved in their movements by responding to their struggles for liberation and self-determination in empowering ways.

Social workers can draw on the principles of feminist social action as they work with women in their communities. These principles take into account the specifics of the social context within which women live and ensure that women develop their own agendas for action. In other words, the client–social worker relationship is based on social workers becoming professionals who are at the service of women, instead of experts who tell women what to do. Sensitivity to the rich diversity of women's lives and support for them in fulfilling their needs rests at the heart of the modern social development process (Sen & Grown, 1987). Moreover, by working with women in their social context, social workers can assist in the creation of a more just world for children, men, and women. The social worker of tomorrow needs to acquire the relevant intellectual, listening, and empowering skills today. Social work education should ensure that these skills become the substance of both theory and practice in the social work curriculum. The "added-on" approach to women is inadequate for the purpose. Therefore there is urgent need to respond to the challenge that social development raises for the social work profession.

REFERENCES

Ahmad, B. (1990). *Black perspectives in social work.* Birmingham, England: Venture Press.

Amos, V., & Parmar, P. (1984). Challenging imperial feminism. *Feminist Review, 17,* 3–19.

Armitage, A. (1995). *Comparing the policy of aboriginal assimilation: Australia, Canada and New Zealand.* Vancouver: University of British Columbia Press.

Bald, S. R. (1995). Coping with marginality: South Asian women migrants in Britain. In M. H. Marchand & J. L. Parpart (Eds.), *Feminism, postmodernism, development* (pp. 110–126). London: Routledge.

Behrendt, L. (1996, Spring). At the back of the class, at the front of the class: Experiences as an Aboriginal student and Aboriginal teacher. *Feminist Review, 52,* 27–35.

Bhavani, K. K. (1993). Racism. In D. Richardson & V. Robinson (Eds.), *Reading women's studies.* London: Macmillan.

Bolger, S., Corrigan, P., Davis, J., & Frost, N. (1981). *Towards socialist welfare practice.* London: Macmillan.

Boserup, E. (1970). *Women's role in economic development.* New York: St. Martin's and George Allen and Unwin.

Bowl, R. (1985). *Changing the nature of masculinity: A task for social work* (Monograph). Norwich, England: University of East Anglia.

Bozalek, V. (1996, July). *Beyond feminist standpoint epistemology.* Paper presented at the 28th International Association of Schools of Social Work Congress, City University, Hong Kong.

Burden, D. S. & Gottlieb, N. (Eds.). (1987). *The woman client: Providing human services in a changing world.* London: Tavistock.

Carby, H. (1982). White women listen! Black feminism and the boundaries of sisterhood. In Centre for Contemporary Cultural Studies (Ed.), *The empire strikes back.* London: Hutchinson.

Chowdhry, C. (1995). Engendering development? Women in development (WID) in international development regimes. In M. H. Marchand & J. L. Parpart (Eds.), *Feminism, postmodernism, development* (pp. 26–41). London: Routledge.

Collins, P. H. (1990). *Black feminist thought.* London: Routledge.

Cook, A., & Kirk, G. (1983). *Greenham women everywhere: Dreams, ideas and action from the women's peace movement.* London: Pluto.

Corrigan, P., & Leonard, P. (1978). *Social work under capitalism.* London: Macmillan.

Dave, A., & Desai, M. (1996, July). *Experiments in integrating women and gender issues in social work education.* Paper presented at the 28th International Association of Schools of Social Work Congress, City University, Hong Kong.

Davis, L. V. (1994). *Building on women's strengths: A social work agenda for the twenty-first century.* New York: Haworth Press.

Devore, W., & Schlesinger, A. (1986). *Ethnic sensitive social work.* London: Macmillan.

Dominelli, L. (1986). Women organising: An analysis of the Greenham Common Women's Peace Movement. *Continuum, 11*(1), 1–19.

Dominelli, L. (1988). *Anti-racist social work.* London: BASW/Macmillan.

Dominelli, L. (1990). *Women and community action.* Birmingham, England: Venture Press.

Dominelli, L. (1991a). Race and gender in social work. In M. Davies (Ed.), *The sociology of social work.* London: Routledge.

Dominelli, L. (1991b). *Women across continents: Feminist comparative social policy.* London: Harvester-Wheatsheaf.

Dominelli, L. (1992). More than a method: Feminist social work. In K. Campbell (Ed.), *Critical feminisms.* Milton Keynes, England: Open University Press.

Dominelli, L. (1997). *Sociology for social work.* London: Macmillan.

Dominelli, L., & McLeod, E. (1989). *Feminist social work.* London: Macmillan.

Frankfort, E. (1972). *Vaginal politics.* New York: Quadrangle Books.

Friedan, B. (1963). *The feminine mystique.* New York: Bell.

Gray, M., Mazibuko, F., & O'Brien, F. (1996). Social work education for social development. *Journal of Social Development in Africa, 11*(1), 33–42.

Haig-Brown, A. (1988). *Indian residential school.* Vancouver: Tillacum Library.

Hanmer, J., & Statham, D. (1987). *Women in social work.* London: Macmillan.

Hanscombe, G., & Forrest, J. (1982). *Rocking the cradle: Lesbian mothers.* London: Sheba Feminist Publishers.

hooks, b. (1994). *Teaching to transgress: Education as the practice of freedom.* London: Routledge.

Hugman, R. (1991). *Professions.* London: Tavistock.

Jayawardena, K. (1995). *The white woman's other burden: Western women and South Asia during British rule.* London: Routledge.

Kaseke, E. (1994, February). *Social work as social development.* Paper presented at the IASSW Board Seminar, the University of Sheffield, Sheffield, England.

Langan, M., & Day, L. (1992). *Women, oppression and social work.* London: Routledge.

Marchand, M. H., & Parpart, J. L. (1995). *Feminism, postmodernism, development.* London: Routledge.

Marchant, H., & Wearing, B. (1986). *Gender reclaimed.* Sidney, Australia: Hale and Iremonger.

Mazuki, B. (1992). Older women. In M. Langan & L. Day (Eds.), *Women, oppression and social work.* London: Routledge.

Meng, L. (1996, July). *Abused women in China.* Paper presented at the 28th International Association of Schools of Social Work Congress, City University, Hong Kong.

Midgley, J. (1995). *Social development: The developmental perspective in social welfare.* Thousand Oaks, CA: Sage Publications.

Mohanty, C. T. (1995). Under Western eyes: Feminist scholarship and colonial discourses. In C. T. Mohanty, A. Russo, & L. Torres (Eds.), *Third World women and the politics of feminism* (pp. 51–80). Bloomington: Indiana University Press.

Morgan, R. (1970). *Sisterhood is powerful.* New York: Vintage.

Morris, J. (1992). *Pride before prejudice: Disability and women.* London: Tavistock.

Oliver, M. (1990). *The politics of disability.* London: Routledge.

Plummer, K. (1981). *The making of the modern homosexual.* London: Hutchinson.

Raissiguier, C. (1995). The construction of marginal identities: Working-class girls of Algerian descent in a French school. In M. H. Marchand & J. L. Parpart (Eds.), *Feminism, postmodernism, development* (pp. 79–93). London: Routledge.

Rush, F. (1980). *The best kept secret: Sexual abuse of children.* New York: McGraw-Hill.

Schön, D. (1983). *The reflective practitioner.* London: Routledge.

Sen, G., & Grown, C. (1987). *Development crises and alternative visions: Third World women's perspectives.* New York: Monthly Review Press.

Sidel, R. (1987). *Women and children last: The plight of poor women in affluent America.* New York: Viking Penguin.

Spender, D. (1970). *Man made language.* London: Routledge.

Walby, S. (1990). *Theorizing patriarchy.* Oxford, England: Basil Blackwell.

Wilson, T. J. (1996). Feminism and institutionalized racism: Inclusion and exclusion at an Australian feminist refuge. *Feminist Review, 52,* 1–26.

7

Ethnic Conflict and Violence in the Modern World

Social Work's Role in Building Peace

VERA MEHTA

Never since World War II have there been so many conflicts in the world, with such a large proliferation of weapons. Between 1945 and 1992, there were 149 major wars which killed more than 23 million people. On an average yearly basis, the number of war fatalities in this period was more than double the number of deaths caused in the 19th century and seven times greater than the number of deaths in 18th-century wars (Sivard, 1993). War and political upheavals have been tearing entire countries apart from Bosnia and Herzegovina, to Cambodia, to Rwanda. This vortex of violence is sucking in ever-larger numbers of adults and children, so much so that entire generations have grown up in the midst of brutal armed conflicts. At the end of 1995, conflicts had been continuing in Angola for more than 30 years, in Afghanistan for 17 years, in Sri Lanka for 11 years, in Somalia for 7 years, and in Sudan for nearly 35 years.

The world of the future will be even more complex. Local conflicts will be more likely and, with modern warfare technology, more lethal. Human carnage, brutalities, and atrocities will defy all imagination. The civilian casualties in World War I were about 5 percent, and the civilian death count rose to 50 percent in World War II (Ahlstrom, 1991, pp. 8, 19). Modern warfare now takes a toll of civilians as high as 90 percent of all casualties, the majority of whom are women and children. There is an urgent need for action: Peacekeeping and peace building, therefore, represent the

Vera Mehta is Special Assistant to the Special Representative of the Secretary-General of the United Nations for FYR of Macedonia. The views expressed in this chapter are solely those of the author and should not be interpreted as the official position of the United Nations.

most concerted effort the international community can make in regulating conflict.

No single government or regional intergovernmental body today, however resourceful, can be expected to contain, let alone resolve, the enormous range of security problems that now confront the world community. If there is to be any meaningful response, it can only be one that is based on a cooperative and multilateral approach. Today much greater attention is given to anticipating and preventing disputes, conflicts, or crises, than on reacting after the event or to situations that have already deteriorated. With a preventive response, conflicts can be reduced or more effectively contained and, consequently, human suffering and tragedies greatly minimized. Conflicts can be resolved more expeditiously, with much less time, cost, and personnel. Despite constraints of resources, the United Nations, through its Security Council, has been and is the main organization capable of developing and mobilizing peacekeeping and peace building as a global cooperative security response. It is also the major organization concerned with war victims, which is especially important because the lives of millions of people are affected in any one conflict.

This chapter presents an overview of global conflicts and conflict prevention and discusses the role of the social work profession in their regard. The realities speak for the urgency of its response. World wars and conflicts, with their complications of ethnicity, dynamics, and potentially explosive nature, lead to untold human tragedy and provide the context in which social work and social welfare interventions can be undertaken. Shifts in the philosophy of international peacekeeping and peace-building efforts are occurring, with emphasis today on prevention rather than on remedial measures.

THE GLOBAL SCENARIO OF CONFLICTS

No fewer than 160 violent and potentially violent domestic and international conflicts confront humankind around the world. Colijn, Jongman, Rusman, and Schmid (1994) stated that in 1993 there were 15 conflicts in the Americas, 12 in the Middle East, 21 in Europe, 31 in Asia, 33 in the former Soviet Union, and 48 in Africa. At least 32 of the conflicts in 28 locations were outright wars according to the generally accepted definition of war. In another 69 conflicts, violence was more sporadic and less intense. The remaining 59 confrontations were serious disputes in which one of the parties involved threatened to use violence, deployed military troops, or made a show of force in the disputed area.

In 1995 there were 22 ongoing wars: 11 on the African continent, 3 in Europe, 5 in the Middle East, 1 in the Americas, and 2 in Asia. In addition, there were 39 low-intensity conflicts and 40 serious disputes. High-intensity conflicts (of more than 1,000 fatalities per year) have decreased since 1993, with a shift to more low-intensity conflicts. The United Nations currently has peacekeeping operations in 17 conflict zones, with regional intergovernmental organizations involved in five of them. Many other conflicts receive no peacekeeping aid, and, consequently, the numbers of both the internally displaced and external refugees have escalated since the end of the Cold War (Schmid, 1994b).

The new era that began in the aftermath of the Cold War and the disappearance of the bipolar nuclear strategic balance was only a prelude to a new kind of turbulence and disorder. There were unprecedented and unanticipated outbursts of conflict in many parts of the globe that stemmed from the resurgence of ethnonationalism. Some ethnic groups were and are still prepared to pursue their aims of self-determination within the framework of existing states, essentially claiming human rights protection as minorities. Many others, however, will not be satisfied until their nations become states, thus causing the fragmentation of existing states. The post–Cold War period has, in fact, unleashed a vast array of security problems in the transition phase of newly established republics.

None of these wars were wars between states, but they have drawn other nations into the conflict to support or oppose them. The last year of the Cold War, 1989, saw the highest figures of the decade: 36 conflicts in 32 locations. In the period from 1989 to 1994, South America and Central America reported the sharpest declines, followed by Africa and then Asia. Europe is the only region with a trend toward increased conflicts since 1990: Out of the breakup and disintegration of the former Yugoslavia and the Soviet Union, 21 new nations have emerged, each with its own potential conflicts.

Ethnicity and Ethnic Conflicts

Ethnicity is a shared cultural identity with a range of distinctive behavioral and, sometimes, linguistic features, which are passed on through socialization from one generation to another. There are never clear cultural or geographic boundaries to mark the limits of ethnic groups, even though many people regard ethnicity as though it were naturally determined. An ethnic community can be understood as a unit of population that shares a common proper name, myths of common ancestry, historical memories, and one or more distinctive elements of culture, such as language or festivities.

It also includes an association with a given territory and a sense of social solidarity.

For better or for worse—probably for worse—ethnicity has become, once again, a major organizing principle for group activities. Political mobilization takes place around ethnic markers, and political parties are no more than ethnic parties in some countries. When such a party attains power, it is likely to act in ways that favor members of its own ethnic group over others. Some derive privileges on the basis of ascription and not achievement, and others feel discriminated against—thus, a source of group conflict is born. "Us-versus-them" and "in-group–out-group" thinking begins to emerge (Schmid, 1995b). Such political parties claim rights for themselves on ethnic bases rather than on sound long-term ideological and programmatic policies and agendas geared toward national development.

Ethnicity can be understood as a

> psychological need for a sense of belonging, as a framework of social organization, and, most important, as a political and economic resource, a major factor in the distribution of power and wealth. A group may emphasize its ethnicity when it is useful and downplay it when it is seen as a handicap. Ethnic conflict is usually defensive or opportunistic, a tool for political mobilization aimed at preserving or capturing resources. (Stavenhagen, 1992)

Modernization theory had assumed that ethnicity was a disappearing principle of social organization, but a revival of the ethnic principle has occurred for any of several reasons. One hypothesis is that the stress of an achievement-oriented society is too high for some segments of the population. The appeal to racism is based partly on the fear of losing out in the face of fierce social competition. The organization of social discontent by ethnically oriented politicians has often been successful; ethnic nationalism often is used as a mobilizing resource by discredited politicians to keep or return to power. The mobilization of ethnicity is also an instrument used by power brokers to create new loyalties.

Why is ethnicity such a conflict-prone issue? Ethnic tensions and resulting instability may tempt outside powers to intervene to maximize their self-interest. When an ethnic group is spread over more than one state but is a majority in one, ethnic strife arising in one state can spill over into another. Conflict can arise in situations where a dominant group in one state is separated from compatriots who are a minority in another. Disaffected ethnic groups have been known to resort to terrorism in their efforts to attain their objectives (Taras, 1993), and there is a new cadre of what may be described as "ethnic entrepreneurs" emerging for their own gain.

Ethnic conflicts are not only battles between contending armies but also battles of brother against brother. They can be complex struggles between the military and civilians or between contending groups of armed civilians. They are as likely to be fought in villages and suburban streets as anywhere else. In this case, the enemy camp is all around and distinctions between combatant and noncombatant fade away in the suspicions and confusions of daily strife. Families are not only likely to get caught in the cross fire; they also are often deliberate targets. The escalation from ethnic superiority to "ethnic cleansing" and then subsequently to genocide can become an irresistible process. Killing adults is not enough. Future generations of the enemy, their children, must also be eliminated (McGarry & O'Leary, 1993). These are chronic forms of social conflict, and their violent repercussions will be felt for years or decades to come because they are built on hatred and revenge that can erupt even after many years or generations.

The Toll of Suffering: A Human Tragedy

Recent technological advances in warfare have significantly heightened its dangers and devastating effects for humankind. Schmid (1994a) has estimated that during the past decade, 2 million children were killed and 4.5 million disabled. Twelve million have been left homeless, and more than 1 million orphaned or separated from their parents. In addition, some 10 million have been psychologically traumatized. In Sarajevo, one of every 30 children has been killed, and one of every four wounded. At least half of the people uprooted by the waves of violence have been children. They are classified as displaced within their own countries and as refugees by other countries. The total number of uprooted people is currently approximately 53 million—one of every 115 people on earth has been forced into flight (United Nations Children's Fund [UNICEF], 1995b). Because three-quarters of these refugees have migrated from one developing country to another, enormous strain is placed on the meager resources of these countries.

One of the most deplorable occurrences in recent years has been the increasing use of young children as soldiers. In 25 countries, thousands of children younger than age 16 have fought in wars because of the proliferation of light weapons, deliberate recruitment, and the military becoming a way of life for children who are abandoned and made destitute by warfare. In 1988 alone, child soldiers numbered as many as 200,000 (UNICEF,

1995a). Unaccompanied minors account for 5 percent or more of refugee populations because children are lost, separated, or orphaned in the panic of flight. In Rwanda at the end of 1994, an estimated 114,000 children had been separated from their families, according to a 1995 UNICEF survey (UNICEF, 1994). In addition, the old and disabled are left behind. Unable to flee with their families, they are most likely doomed to destitution and loneliness for the rest of their lives.

Women and children have been imprisoned, tortured, and raped as a strategy of war, as part of collective punishment of families and entire communities, or as a means of extracting information. The treatment of child prisoners is a matter of concern, particularly in Rwanda where, for the first time in history, children who have been imprisoned are facing trial for genocide. Sexual violence is particularly common in ethnic conflicts, including deliberate policies of raping teenage girls and forcing them to bear the enemies' children. A European Community fact-finding team estimated that more than 20,000 Muslim women have been raped in Bosnia since the fighting broke out in April 1992 (Dodge, 1991; Ressler, 1993; UNICEF, United Nations Development Fund, United Nations Development Fund for Women, 1995). In Rwanda, rape has been systematically used as a weapon of ethnic cleansing to destroy communities. In some raids, virtually every girl who survived an attack by the Hutu government-supported militia was then raped. Many of those who became pregnant were ostracized by their families and community. Some abandoned their babies, and others committed suicide.

Even women and girls who are not physically forced to have sex may still be obliged to trade sexual favors for food, shelter, or physical protection for themselves and their children. Increased rates of sexually transmitted diseases, especially of HIV and AIDS, are therefore inevitable. One factor contributing to the high rate of AIDS in Uganda may be that some women had to trade sex for security during that country's civil war. As a result, the next generation is at an even greater disadvantage as more children are born with AIDS or are orphaned by the disease.

Most of the casualties in wartime have not been injured by bombs, mines, or bullets but have succumbed to starvation or sickness. The lack of food and medical services combined with the stress of flight have killed about 209 times more people than armaments in the African wars. A study of a war zone in Uganda attributed only 2 percent of deaths to violence, whereas 20 percent were caused by disease and 78 percent by hunger (Ressler, 1993; United Nations Development Programme [UNDP], 1994; United Nations Department of Public Information [UNDPI], 1990). Millions suffer from war as resources that could have been invested in development are diverted into amassing armaments. One of the saddest and most distressing realities of our time is that most wars have been fought in precisely those countries that could least afford them.

The majority of deaths result from disruption of the normal production and distribution of food. The manipulation of food supplies has always been a significant tactic of war and, of late, has been used particularly ruthlessly. Scorched-earth methods are used to destroy food-producing land, and antipersonnel mines are buried in fields to hamper the production of food. Grain stores have been subject to attack, whether by rebel or government forces. War also hinders the distribution of food relief, with the widespread abuse of humanitarian aid. People forced into squalor and deprivation, the characteristic conditions of refugee camps, are vulnerable to illness and hunger. One of the most serious problems is malnutrition. Refugee populations in Somalia, Angola, Liberia, and Sudan have had extremely high mortality rates. In 1994, a cholera epidemic killed as many as 50,000 people in just one month in the Goma refugee camp in eastern Zaire.

Even water can be a weapon of destruction. War cuts supplies of water, with particular risk in the cities. The long and devastating war in Lebanon had a very damaging effect on the quantity and quality of drinking water. Urban water sources can be contaminated when makeshift cesspools or latrines are used for sewage disposal. Water systems in Sarajevo have been deliberately destroyed to isolate and break down residential neighborhoods. Thirty percent of the pumping system and 60 percent of water mains have been ruined. Parties at war also use attacks on other sections of the health infrastructure, such as hospitals and clinics, as a way of crippling community life.

Many problems of nutrition and health can arise not just from military but also from economic warfare, as the outside world exerts pressure on errant regimes. Sanctions imposed raise the ethical question of whether suffering inflicted on vulnerable groups in the target country is a legitimate means of exerting pressure on political leaders whose behavior is unlikely to be affected by the plight of their victims. The balance sheet of several years of sanctions against certain countries reveals a minimum of political dividends but a high human price, paid primarily by women and children. Sanctions reduce food and water supplies and sanitation. Medical facilities not only face a critical shortage of life-saving drugs and equipment but can also collapse.

It is clear that poverty and lack of development fuel hatred and escalate hostilities. Improvements in such areas as nutrition, health, education, water, sanitation, and family planning would go far to reduce the underlying causes of so many wars. UNDP (1994) has estimated that redirecting just one-quarter of military expenditures in developing countries could provide additional resources to implement most of a program aimed at primary health care covering the entire population, immunization for all children, elimination of severe malnutrition, provision of safe drinking water for all, universal primary education, reduction of illiteracy, and family planning by 2000.

Of all the weapons that have accumulated over years of war, few are more persistent than land mines and virtually all combatants make use of them. Since 1975, more than 1 million have exploded and are currently thought to be killing 800 people a month. There seems little prospect of any end to this carnage. In 64 countries around the world, there are an estimated 110 million land mines still lodged in the ground—waiting (United Nations, 1994a). They remain active for decades. As one Khmer Rouge general put it, a land mine is a perfect soldier, "Ever courageous, never sleeps, never misses."

Adults and especially children hardly survive and, if they do, they suffer physical impairment for life with injuries to or loss of lower extremities. Blindness and disfigurement from shrapnel are common. Most of the mines are planted in countries where few painkilling medications are available, let alone artificial limbs. Land mines bring lingering economic and social costs as well. They hinder the flow of goods and people and put large areas of agricultural land out of production. Their presence contributes to the permanent militarization of daily life, with mines commonly used for fishing, as property security devices, or even to settle domestic disputes. They pose a constant threat to people walking, planting crops, and herding animals and to children just playing in the fields.

Ironically, these weapons can cost as little as US$3 each to manufacture and as much as US$1,000 each to clear at an extremely slow pace of no more than 20 to 50 square meters per day (UNICEF, 1996). The international community is slow in realizing the implications of a world studded with land mines. As of now, a "de-mining deficit" of 1.9 million mines adds US$1.4 billion to the future cost of clearance.

GLOBAL SECURITY AND PEACEKEEPING

As part of the new political climate following the end of the Cold War, the major powers have demonstrated a greater political will to use the United Nations to seek solutions to conflicts. Between 1945 and 1988, the United Nations initiated 13 peacekeeping operations. In 1988, as the Cold War was coming to an end, the Security Council met 55 times and adopted 20 resolutions. In 1994, the Security Council met 165 times and adopted 77 resolutions. In 1988, there were five peacekeeping operations, with some 9,000 troops deployed, but from 1988 to 1994, 22 new peacekeeping operations were approved. In July 1995 approximately 65,000 troops, 17,000 police, and 6,000 civilian personnel were serving in 17 peacekeeping operations around the world (Crosset, 1995; Ressler, 1993; Sollenberg & Wallenstein, 1995; United Nations, 1994b; UNDP, 1994; UNICEF, 1993; UNICEF, 1994). The service to the cause of peace by more than 650,000 soldiers and civilians since 1948 was formally recognized in 1988 when United Nations peacekeeping forces were awarded the Nobel Peace Prize (UNDPI, 1990).

Despite these accomplishments, the financial constraints on the United Nations and the limited enthusiasm for peacekeeping operations among its Member States have shifted the burden onto nongovernment organizations (NGOs), which together spend some US$4 billion a year in providing relief and numerous other services. However, NGOs cannot play the role of nation states and lack the means to exercise international pressure and sanctions and thus bring about conflict resolution on their own.

There also has been a qualitative change in the nature and functions of a number of recent peacekeeping operations. They are now often used to assist in more ambitious attempts to reach conflict resolution and enable countries to move toward social reconstruction, development, and progress. Mandates have become more complex, and the number, size, and composition of these peacekeeping operations are of quite a different order than those of the last 40 years in the history of the United Nations.

Preventive Diplomacy and Social Development

An Agenda for Peace, a report issued by United Nations Secretary-General Boutros Boutros-Ghali in 1992, initiated a major international discussion of the role of the United Nations and the international community, in general, in ensuring peace for humankind in the last decade of the 20th century and beyond. The report focused on preventive diplomacy, peacemaking, and peacekeeping. Preventive diplomacy is an evolving concept, which, in its classical form, requires measures to build confidence. It needs early warning based on information gathering and fact finding, and it may also involve preventive deployment and, in some situations, demilitarized zones (Boutros-Ghali, 1992).

Preventive deployment, a part of preventive diplomacy, is a relatively new concept for the United Nations. It was given prominence by the Secretary-General's advocacy in *An Agenda for Peace* and by its recent application for the first, and so far only, time in the former Yugoslav Republic of Macedonia, where the United Nations Preventive Deployment Force (UNPREDEP) has been instituted. The essence of this strategy is a preventive military response accompanied by a political and diplomatic intervention. It involves positioning troops, military observers, and related civilian personnel on one or both sides of the border between entities that are in dispute. Preventive action can also be used where there is an emergent conflict, with the primary objective of deterring the escalation of that situation into armed conflict. Associated objectives may be to calm communities by monitoring law and order and general conditions and to render other forms of assistance to the local authorities and population.

Preventive diplomacy, therefore, involves government and non-government diplomatic, political, economic, military, or other efforts that are taken deliberately at an early stage to keep states or communal groups from threatening or using armed force or coercion as the way to settle political disputes that arise from the destabilizing effects of national and international change. It aims to discourage or minimize hostilities, reduce tensions, address differences, create channels for resolution, and alleviate insecurities and material conditions that tempt violence. Conceptually, preventive diplomacy falls between "normal routine diplomacy" in a relatively stable international environment such as in the context of development cooperation or trade negotiations, on the one hand, and "crisis or war diplomacy" on the other (Lund, 1994).

The sequel to *An Agenda for Peace* was *An Agenda for Development,* in which the Secretary-General stated that only sustained efforts to resolve underlying socioeconomic, cultural, and humanitarian problems can place an achieved peace on a durable foundation (Boutros-Ghali, 1993). Social and economic development can be a secure basis for lasting peace and can be as valuable in preventing conflicts as in healing the wounds after conflicts have occurred. The Security Council urges states to support the efforts of the United Nations system with regard to preventive and postconflict peace-building activities and, in this context, to provide assistance for the economic and social development of countries, especially those that have suffered or are suffering from conflicts (Statement of the President of the Security Council, 1995).

As a result, many new developmental and humanitarian activities have been added to the military and political posts of preventive diplomacy.

These programs initiated in the social sector will foster socioeconomic stability and social integration among diverse ethnic communities.

SOCIAL RECONSTRUCTION AND PREVENTIVE ACTION

The profession of social work is ideally suited to work in the emergency relief and rehabilitation programs needed in the early and midcrisis phases of ethnic conflict. It should also play an important role in postdisaster reconstruction and in approaches to preventive diplomacy and preventive action. Social workers in these roles can use their existing knowledge and skills, but they will also need new knowledge and additional skills to be most effective.

Social work in emergency relief, mid- or postdisaster social reconstruction, and preventive action requires various levels of intervention: the world community, a country, regions, districts, communities, families, and individuals. Increasingly, the profession will have to assume a proactive stance along with other professional disciplines and sectors and other key actors such as the military; governments; the United Nations; regional organizations, such as the Organization of American States, the Organization of African Unity, the Organization for Security and Cooperation in Europe, the Arab League, the Organization of the Islamic Conference, the Association of South East Asian States; and other intergovernment and nongovernment organizations and international aid and human rights agencies.

Relief work with individuals and families involves intensive counseling; physical, medical, and psychological rehabilitation; tracing missing family members across borders and reunifying them; and repatriating and resettling refugees. It also includes empowering victims to exercise their rights and organize collaborative enterprises. Because there are ever-increasing numbers of civilian war victims to be reached and relatively few social work professionals available, group and community methods must be used to provide these services and a new cadre of personnel must be created by training community aides and using indigenous leadership.

Delivery of services can be targeted at frontline grassroots intervention or at the decision, policy-making, planning, and implementation levels of operation. These units and levels of intervention are not mutually exclusive, and strategies have to be sufficiently versatile to be effective in all of them. War zones demand a multifocal social work practitioner equipped with generic and integrated methods and skills. There is also scope for the exercise of more specialized skills in particular fields of services delivery, from trauma counseling and rehabilitation of war victims to community development with self-help initiatives accompanied by macroeconomic and social policy strategies. The delivery of services range across a wide continuum of therapeutic and developmental approaches, providing an opportunity for the practice of all methods of social work and social development.

Numerous services are needed for relief and reconstruction, and many United Nations operations with their specialized agencies now involve a large civilian dimension in addition to military roles. They include rendering emergency humanitarian aid; demanding large-scale administrative management for millions of victims; providing medical and health services; improvising schools, shelters, and specialized rehabilitation; counseling victims of trauma; and organizing telephone hotlines. In the developmental sector, the focus is on reconstruction and developmental assistance, monitoring violations of human rights, mediating, fostering interethnic dialogue, institution building, strengthening government infrastructure, national capacity building in all spheres, and promoting education for peace and nonviolent conflict resolution. Social workers have an important role to play in these programs. However, the challenge is to work in settings of hardship where there is no normal provision of resources, institutions, and personnel.

Social Work as Part of Preventive Action

The social work profession can work toward just structures, equitable distribution of resources and services, and fulfillment of basic needs to prevent ethnic tensions and conflicts from arising. Social workers should learn to work in the field of early warning and use the tools that have been devised. For example, early warning models (EWMs) have largely been used to forecast ecological disasters, such as droughts or storms. Only recently have EWMs been extended to predict other human disasters such as conflicts or population movements. Although it is unlikely that an EWM will ever be able to predict the exact date of outbreak of such disasters, it is a tool for alerting the international community to conditions in countries and patterns of events and actions that could easily lead to a crisis. This information can also be used to indicate the potential points for intervention. It provides a base for the development of scenarios and strategic alternative responses to prevent or inhibit the escalation of the factors most likely to cause conflict and refugee migration (Lund, 1994).

The ongoing capacity to formulate and mobilize preventive measures in particular places and at particular times requires a range of appropriate strategies. These include programs and resources as varied as official diplomacy, nonofficial problem-solving and conflict resolution workshops, preventive deployment of peace keepers, and targeted socioeconomic assistance. The repertoire of usual prevention alternatives can be expanded and disseminated especially in the human and social dimensions—processes in which social work has an important role to play.

Comparative-case study research has begun on the factors that explain differing outcomes, and this will be continued by those committed to peace building. Useful preliminary generalizations, such as timing and sequencing of third-party preventive actions or domestic governance arrangements, most conducive to dispute settlements that avoid violence, are being derived by comparing apparent successes with obvious failures. For example, national political disputes with ethnic overtones, such as those arising recently in the early phases of democratization and transition in Central and Eastern Europe and Africa, are more amenable to resolution if third parties act in a relatively concerted way with a number of incentives and disincentives. Peaceful resolution can be sought if intervention occurs when the contending parties have begun to voice their conflicting interests, but before either side has publicly mobilized a political constituency or begun to arm their followers.

Another important activity is to provide technical assistance to governments in the social sector in their efforts to formulate new social policies that reduce unemployment and create more job opportunities, overcome poverty, and foster social integration. Social integration involves ensuring the participation of all ethnic groups in the life of a nation, with equality of access in all social provisions to the expertise of social workers. To achieve this, efforts will also have to be made to strengthen government infrastructure and national capacity building of local professionals in spheres of service delivery at the micro and macro levels; policy review, formulation, and change; implementation and administration of programs; monitoring and evaluation; research; and further education through formal and nonformal systems.

The building of a civil society in nations and regions with the potential for ethnic conflict also is an important objective of timely preventive action. Social workers are well suited to assist local populations in this process by facilitating proactive social interventions, organizing community development projects, and creating new or strengthening existing nonprofit organizations that can defuse tensions and aid in laying stable foundations of society. Social workers can also provide assistance in the decentralization of services provision, so that local authorities, populations, and different ethnic groups have a real sense of influence over resources and services.

The human dimension, pursued by UNPREDEP as the third pillar of its peacekeeping mission, yields manifold dividends as a major supplement to other effective political and military prevention techniques. It can be regarded as an important confidence-building measure between the people and the authorities of the host country, on the one hand, and the peacekeeping mission and other international entities, on the other, thus helping to resolve sensitive political and interethnic problems. Hence, efforts at timely socioeconomic and humane interventions place a preventive operation in the forefront of a process of positive change, rather than in the role of passive observer (Sokalski, 1996).

A large number of catalytic activities in the social development, welfare, and policy sectors have been undertaken to demonstrate to different institutions in the host country how to use duly approved international standards to pursue their own national social policy and integration programs. The host country institutions also benefit from the experience gained in the implementation of these standards by other countries on their way to civil society. Consequently, the United Nations has been involved in a preventive project for which there is no parallel (Sokalski, 1996). Its model peace building has provided unlimited scope for the various specializations of social work to demonstrate their competence and skills, and it serves as a blueprint for future conflict prevention and resolution.

Challenges for Social Work Education

Social workers have the basic knowledge and skills for professional practice mainly in times of peace. However, additional training and experience are essential to prepare them effectively to work in zones of potential and actual violence that results from ethnic conflicts. New competence is needed for making political analyses and achieving a full understanding of the complex conditions that contribute to conflict. Specialized skills are needed for monitoring and reporting humanitarian concerns and violations of human rights and to contribute to the planning and implemention of preventive action and peace-building programs. Social workers need competence in the increasingly recognized and effective second track of preventive diplomacy through the interventions of nonpolitical actors such as nongovernment organizations, experts in peace research, academics, and development specialists and practitioners, all of whom have firsthand information about the field.

There are many curriculum areas where additional or specialized course content is needed if social workers are to be adequately prepared to work at preventive or postdisaster reconstruction efforts. An orientation toward the United Nations system and its specialized agencies; international relations; the mandates of regional organizations; international regimes, conventions, declarations, standards, and rights or ethnic and national minority groups, including different religious, cultural, and linguistic groups, is a prime requirement. Only with such information will social workers be able to work effectively with international, regional, and national commissions and tribunals. Work with the media is a capability that must be acquired as well. A systematic effort is needed to develop case studies in the dynamics of power and ethnic conflict and to expand the professional literature that addresses conflict prevention and resolution and developmental interventive strategies.

Student field placements can be considered in human rights organizations, specialized agencies of the United Nations system and international aid agencies, their own countries, and elsewhere in the conflict zones. The few social workers who are currently engaged in this work could serve as field instructors, visiting lecturers, and resource specialists to help build the educational programs for professional practice in this setting. Research projects on war-related themes, mid- and postdisaster social reconstruction, and monitoring and evaluation techniques should be included as topics for potential group assignments and dissertations.

Finally, institutions of social work education and professional organizations of social workers at the national, regional, and international levels can be directly involved in human rights work, projects of peace building, and technical assistance along the vast continuum of pre-, mid-, and post-conflict settings.

CONCLUSION

The underlying tensions that eventually erupt in violence are often easy enough to identify. There is increasing awareness of conditions that generate marginalization, produce vulnerability, exploit differences, and exacerbate tensions. Thus, it is clear that treating root causes is the only answer for preventing conflict. It could be argued that many countries have not fallen victim to widespread violence precisely because they have pursued policies of more equitable economic and social development and effective social integration.

The use of force has proven unfit to resolve conflicts. It destroys much that is valuable in the economy and in society and does not create conditions for cooperation. Decentralization of authority with all groups sharing power has worked in many instances. Democratic forms of government hold out opportunities for such diffusion of power. The enlargement of social and economic opportunities tends to reduce conflicts as all groups perceive the benefits of life together. Physical infrastructure that ends isolation and integrates communities into a larger social interaction would greatly help movement in these directions (United Nations, 1994b).

Many ethnic and religious conflicts have drawn world attention. One part of the international effort to alleviate them is concerned with mitigating the disastrous consequences of violence and destruction. An inherently more difficult component concerns finding political solutions to conflicts, and currently both regional and worldwide intergovernment organizations are engaged in this task. Voluntary international organizations also have played an outstanding role in humanitarian, developmental, and peace-building work in the war-torn areas of the world. The time has now come for preventing conflicts through preventive deployment, diplomacy, and political action accompanied by efforts to establish social peace and stability. The United Nations Preventive Deployment Force has demonstrated the value of close links among the military, political, and social dimensions in peacekeeping operations in the future. Such intermediaries—with a focus also on prevention and social development—offer increased opportunities for social work to become more actively involved in peace building as well as peacekeeping.

No part of this planet remains in isolation. Peace is everybody's concern. Social workers, who stand for human dignity, freedom, and justice, have a professional obligation to contribute to global security and international cooperation.

For their assistance, the author thanks Professor Dr. Alex Schmid, Director, Interdisciplinary Research Programme on Root Causes of Human Rights Violations, Leiden University, The Netherlands; and the UNICEF Skopje Project Office.

REFERENCES

Ahlstrom, C. (1991). *Casualties of conflict: Report for the world campaign for the protection of victims of war.* Uppsala, Sweden: Department of Peace and Conflict Research.

Boutros-Ghali, B. (1992). *An agenda for peace: Preventive diplomacy, peace-making and peacekeeping.* New York: United Nations.

Boutros-Ghali, B. (1993). *An agenda for development* (Document A/48/935). New York: United Nations.

Colijn, K., Jongman, B., Rusman, P., & Schmid, A. (1994). *Wars, low intensity conflicts and serious disputes: A global inventory of current confrontations.* Leiden, The Netherlands: Interdisciplinary Research Programme on Root Causes of Human Rights Violations, Leiden University.

Crosset, B. (1995, January 6). UN chief chides Security Council on military missions. *New York Times.*

Dodge, C. P. (1991). Child soldiers of Uganda and Mozambique. In C. P. Dodge, M. Raudalen, & S. Forlag (Eds.), *Reaching children in war: Sudan, Uganda and Mozambique.* Uppsala, Sweden: Sigma Forlag.

Lund, M. (1994). *Preventive diplomacy and American foreign policy: A guide for the post Cold War era.* Washington, DC: United States Institute for Peace.

McGarry, J., & O'Leary, B. (Eds.). (1993). *The politics of ethnic conflict regulation.* New York: Routledge.

Ressler, E. M. (1993). *Children in war: A guide to the provision of services.* New York: United Nations Children's Fund.

Schmid, A. (1994a). *Editorial on ethnic conflicts.* Leiden, The Netherlands: Interdisciplinary Research Programme on Root Causes of Human Rights Violations, Leiden University.

Schmid, A. (1994b). *1995 statistics on wars, conflicts and disputes.* Leiden, The Netherlands: Interdisciplinary Research Programme on Root Causes of Human Rights Violations, Leiden University.

Schmid, A. (1995a). *Ethnic conflict resolution.* Leiden, The Netherlands: Interdisciplinary Research Programme on Root Causes of Human Rights Violations, Leiden University.

Schmid, A. (1995b). *Typology of conflicts.* Leiden, The Netherlands: Interdisciplinary Research Programme on Root Causes of Human Rights Violations, Leiden University.

Sivard, R. (1993). *World military and social expenditures.* Washington, DC: World Priorities.

Sokalski, H. (1996, October). *Preventive diplomacy: The need for a comprehensive approach, Skopje.* Paper presented at an international workshop, An Agenda for Preventive Diplomacy: Theory and Practice, Skopje, former Yugoslav Republic of Macedonia.

Sollenberg, M., & Wallenstein, P. (1995). Major armed conflicts in armaments, disarmament and international security. In *Yearbook 1995, Swedish International Peace Research Institute, Uppsala.* Oxford, England: Oxford University Press.

Statement of the President of the Security Council. (1995, February 22). New York: United Nations.

Stavenhagen, R. (1992). *The ethnic question.* Tokyo: United Nations University Press.

Taras, R. (1993). Making sense of matrioshka nationalism. In I. Bremmer & R. Taras (Eds.), *Nations' politics in the Soviet successor states.* Cambridge, England: Cambridge University Press.

United Nations. (1994a). *Assistance in mine clearance* (Report of the Secretary-General, Document A/49/357). New York: Author.

United Nations. (1994b). *World social situation in the 1990s.* New York: Author.

United Nations Children's Fund. (1993, June-July). *Psychosocial programme emergency operations in former Yugoslavia kit* [UNICEF reference to data collected in Sarajevo in June and July 1993].

United Nations Children's Fund. (1994, October). Overview of recent UNICEF activities. In *Emergency fund raising kit* (Update No. 4). New York: Author.

United Nations Children's Fund. (1995a). *Complete estimates from a diversity of sources.* New York: Author.

United Nations Children's Fund. (1995b). *The state of the world's children.* New York: Author.

United Nations Children's Fund, United Nations Development Fund, & United Nations Development Fund for Women. (1995). Women in armed conflict. In *Convention on the elimination of all forms of discrimination against women.* New York: Author.

United Nations Department of Public Information. (1990). *The blue helmets: A review of United Nations peacekeeping.* New York: Author.

United Nations Department of Public Information. (1995, January). Peace-keeping: Answers at your fingertips. In *About the United Nations.* New York: Author.

United Nations Development Programme. (1994). *Human development report 1994.* New York: Author.

8

Social Work with Refugees

The Growing International Crisis

RODRECK MUPEDZISWA

The refugee problem is perhaps the most serious crisis facing humankind today. The numbers of people who have been displaced from their places of abode have increased rapidly in recent times and have now reached unprecedented proportions. Although the problems refugees experience have not changed much over the years, the refugee problem itself has become much more serious. The enormous growth in refugee numbers, the complexity of the political situations that account for much of the problem, the phenomenon of internal displacement, the prevalence of violence against refugees, the hostilities they experience in host countries, and many other factors have compounded the problem.

Although refugees are often believed to be entirely dependent on international assistance, they are capable of helping themselves. They often re-create their communities while in exile, and they frequently establish organizations to represent their interests, exert political pressures on host governments, and actively campaign for improvements in their conditions. They also support each other economically. Studies have documented the economic benefits that accrue when ethnic minority groups, including refugees, band together (Light, 1972; Sowell, 1981).

Although the use of these survival strategies suggests that refugees are not helpless, they do face enormous hardships, serious material deprivations, and major psychological trauma. They frequently lose close family members and are the victims of brutal violence; they often encounter hostility from host nations and indifference from host governments as well. In addition, many refugees remain in exile for long periods: Some remain in exile for their entire lives and suffer the long-term effects of being displaced from their homes, communities, and friends.

These realities pose a great challenge to policymakers and demand the greater involvement of professional social workers in the field. Although social workers have been engaged in refugee work for many years, their role has been limited and much more needs to be done to promote their active involvement. Because the refugee problem has an obvious international dimension, it offers a special challenge to social workers who are involved in international activities. Social work has a critical role to play in providing services that will enhance the welfare of refugees throughout the world.

THE REFUGEE PROBLEM IN THE MODERN WORLD

Although refugees are generally understood to be people who have fled their own countries and crossed international borders to escape political persecution, this is not always the case. Today it is recognized that refugees include displaced people who may not have physically crossed national borders—nor is it always the case that refugees have fled from political oppression. It is now more widely accepted that the conventional definition of refugees is inadequate and needs to be broadened to include people who have fled conditions of general violence. Sometimes these conditions involve their own governments, but often they arise when governments cannot control outbreaks of violence directed at particular groups of people. In addition, it is recognized that people are displaced by environmental and economic adversities. This broader approach suggests that internally displaced people should also be considered refugees.

The total number of refugees worldwide has grown steadily over the years. Unfortunately, statistical data on the subject are only estimates, and often they are inaccurate (Rogers & Copeland, 1993). In addition, the data are seldom suited to the needs of service providers, and this complicates refugee protection efforts. The need for improved data is critical if services for refugees are to be improved.

In 1964 it was estimated that there were 1.4 million international refugees in the world. In 1970 the figure grew to 2.5 million. By 1980 it had reached 5 million, and in 1990, it exceeded 14 million. By 1993 the number of refugees was estimated to have reached 17 million (United Nations High Commissioner for Refugees [UNHCR], 1995). Put another way, one in every 130 people in the world today has been forced into flight and exile.

These data relate only to refugees who have crossed international borders. In addition to these figures, it is estimated that in 1993 there were approximately 24 million internally displaced people who had fled from violence and persecution but had not crossed international borders (U.S. Committee for Refugees, 1993).

It is often assumed that refugees from Africa, Asia, and Central and South America flee to the Western industrial countries. This is not correct. The large majority of refugees from the developing nations have fled to other developing countries. Migration patterns confirm that a disproportionate share of refugees flee to the world's poorest countries (Black, 1993; Leopold & Harrell-Bond, 1994). Similarly, refugees from Eastern Europe have generally remained in Europe. Although the media have reported that several European countries have experienced an influx of asylum seekers from the developing nations during the past decade, the numbers are quite small (Black, 1993).

Trouble spots that generate refugee flows are found throughout the world. For instance, after the Gulf War, 1.8 million Iraqi Kurds fled to the border region of Turkey and to Iran. Recently more than 400,000 refugees flooded into Kenya from Somalia, Sudan, and Ethiopia, and more than 1.2 million victims of the violence in the former Yugoslavia sought refuge in Croatia, Montenegro, Slovenia, and Macedonia. In the industrial nations, a staggering figure of some 3.7 million applicants for sanctuary was recorded in the period from 1983 through 1992 alone.

Statistics show that the refugee problem is becoming more and more intractable. In addition to the traditional refugee-generating countries, there have been notable additions. The disintegration of the former Soviet Union and the former Yugoslavia have had the greatest impact in recent years (Black, 1993). The African continent also has generated many a new influx, largely as a consequence of internal conflict in places such as Rwanda, Mozambique, Angola, and the Horn of Africa (U.S. Committee for Refugees, 1993).

Costs of the Refugee Problem

The international refugee problem confronts humanity with a major challenge. It is full of both human and financial costs. The human costs are related to the effect of the refugee experience on affected individuals. These costs also emerge out of the problems refugees encounter in their host countries. A prolonged stay in exile is particularly costly and imposes a considerable financial burden in terms of the services needed to care for refugees (Rogers & Copeland, 1993). Black (1993) pointed out that the costs of providing for refugees would still be high if all countries allowed asylum seekers to find employment and reduce the need for public assistance.

Many countries today are experiencing difficulty in providing for the large influx of refugees. The developing countries are particularly affected. The situation is compounded by the apparent permanence of certain refugee populations. Through a host of international refugee programs, the international community is obliged to offer protection to refugees. The burden of providing services thus falls on individual countries, but the international community shares in these costs as well. Today international activities in the field of refugee support and protection are coordinated by UNHCR. Some estimates place the international cost of providing for refugees at 10 times the total budget of UNHCR (Widgren, 1990).

Although most countries have accepted the principle that refugees shall not be forcibly sent back to their home countries, this principle has been flouted with impunity in many parts of the world, generating additional human costs and imposing costs on the international community, which is concerned with protecting the rights of refugees. International protection has several pertinent elements. These include admission of refugees to safety, exemption from forcible return, nondiscrimination, and assistance for survival (UNHCR, 1993). The implementation of these commitments involves costs for the international community and for those countries that provide for refugees.

The assistance provided by UNHCR is meant to lessen the burden on countries that receive refugees, but at times the problem is so enormous that international assistance has had a very limited effect. Often the refugees flee from a poor country into a neighboring poor country that cannot afford to provide adequate services for them (Black, 1993). An example is the cost of Mozambican refugees who fled into Malawi. Both countries are among the poorest in the world. The sheer extent of the burden can be appreciated from the fact that at the height of the turmoil, there was one Mozambican refugee for every nine Malawians.

Causes of the Refugee Problem

The reasons people have to flee from their homes basically fall into three categories: political, economic, and environmental. The political factor is probably the single most serious and common cause of refugee movement. It, in turn, is attributable to factors such as political disputes, ethnic conflicts, militarism, and insurgency. Sources of conflict are often oppressive governments or armed opposition groups. Human rights violations are cited by UNHCR as the primary cause for refugee movements. The Shining Path movement in Peru and the Khmer Rouge in Cambodia are two recent examples. At other times, lack of representative political institutions triggers conflicts—examples of this are the recent violence in Somalia, Liberia, and Afghanistan. Superpower involvement has also exacerbated these problems. UNHCR (1993) put it poignantly when it observed that wars, persecution, and intolerance are ancient themes in the human drama and that refugees are the perennial characters in this drama.

Economic tensions have also been identified as a potential source of refugee influx, particularly in the developing world. In some instances bitter disputes occur over certain policies. Some of these disputes may be related to the distribution of resources, particularly in situations of general economic malaise. Although not a major cause of refugee movement itself, economic deprivation interacts with other circumstances to heighten instability and aggravate existing conflicts (UNHCR, 1993). Poverty can certainly exacerbate ethnic and communal tensions and increase the plight of victims of political violence. When people who are in antagonistic relationships are compelled to compete for scarce resources, existing conflicts are likely to intensify. Similarly, conflict can contribute to even higher levels of poverty among low-income people. Today more than 1 billion people in the world live in absolute poverty, and their circumstances deteriorate further when they are faced with political violence. Conflict may disrupt food production and disturb established patterns of economic activity. It also displaces many poor people, who then become destitute. Where food production is disrupted by war, the ensuing famine can trigger a mass migration.

Environmental factors also cause displacement. Environmental refugees have been defined in different ways in the literature, but as McGregor (1993) pointed out, environmental causes of migration are usually compounded by political and economic problems. Nevertheless, natural disasters and other environmental problems in themselves have in the past been a major cause of involuntary population movements. In addition, less dramatic long-term trends, such as desertification and deforestation, may not only damage the ecology but harm established patterns of agriculture so that people are compelled to move and find other forms of livelihood. As UNHCR (1993) noted, the dislocation of the natural resource base, coupled with demographic pressure and chronic poverty, can exacerbate existing political, ethnic, and social tensions and force people to flee.

Examples of areas where environmental difficulties have created refugee movements include the Sahel region of Africa, Mozambique, and the Horn of Africa. In many of these situations, environmental problems have been accompanied by political strife. One of the most dramatic examples of a human-induced environmental problem that has triggered mass population movement was the Chernobyl nuclear disaster. Because of this event, whole towns and communities have been abandoned. However, victims of these and other disasters do not normally qualify as refugees in the strict sense of the term, even though they are in urgent need of assistance from both their governments and the international community.

RESPONDING TO THE REFUGEE PROBLEM

Refugees are not helpless, as has been noted. They are able to adopt survival strategies in adapting to the challenges they face. This is the way refugees have historically coped with the reality of displacement and flight. Although they have often received assistance from the inhabitants of the lands into which they have fled, many refugees apply their own skills and abilities to cope with the problems they face (Leopold & Harrell-Bond, 1994).

Only in this century has the plight of refugees attracted systematic attention. As a result, coherent policies and programs for responding to the problems of refugees have emerged. The formulation of policies and programs of this kind is largely the result of the work of international agencies that have assumed responsibility for responding to the refugee problem. However, social scientists have also contributed to the field by studying the nature and extent of the problem, undertaking research into the causes of displacement, and assisting in the formulation of effective policies for assisting refugees.

International involvement with refugees dates back to 1921, when the League of Nations created the office of High Commissioner for Russian Refugees to assist those who had fled persecution by the Soviet authorities (Leopold & Harrell-Bond, 1994). At that time the international community first recognized that international action was needed to assist refugees. Although individual states had previously assumed this responsibility, the duty to protect refugees was now accepted as an international obligation. This principle governs international policy toward refugees today.

Between 1921 and World War II, the League of Nations created a succession of organizations and ratified various agreements to deal with new refugee situations as they occurred. However, the current laws, norms, and institutions that govern international responses to refugee problems were introduced after World War II, when the United Nations replaced the League of Nations. In 1947 a new body known as the International Refugee Organization (IRO) was established. Its mandate was to protect the 21 million refugees scattered over Europe in the aftermath of the war. In 1951, IRO was replaced by the United Nations High Commissioner for Refugees, which firmly established the notion of international refugee protection. Today UNHCR has the mandate for coordinating refugee protection activities all over the world.

UNHCR provides international leadership in formulating and implementing policies and programs in response to the refugee problem. It has collaborated with governments and other international bodies to deal with the causes of displacement and to facilitate support for asylum seekers. It has been extensively involved in negotiating the repatriation of refugees and a return to conditions of normality conducive to the reintegration of refugees into their home communities, as well as providing relief services to refugees. UNHCR has also been actively engaged in determining which long-term strategies are the most effective in dealing with the problem.

In its efforts to address the plight of refugees, UNHCR has formulated a comprehensive strategy based on five elements: prevention, preparedness, response, protection, and solution (UNHCR, 1993). The first element, prevention, is to prevent displacement from occurring through intervention directed at potential causes of displacement, such as escalating ethnic tensions, increasing conflict or state oppression, and the heightened risks associated with environmental and economic disasters. Of course, prevention does not mean erecting obstacles to refugee movements, but rather addressing both the root and the immediate causes of flight.

Prevention is a highly desirable goal, but it is not always possible to prevent a refugee crisis from occurring. Sometimes the sheer force of political tension is too great to be contained by preventive strategies. Although the international community has often been aware of critical flash points in different parts of the world, it has not always been able or willing to take decisive action to prevent an emergency situation from occurring. The recent crises in the Balkans and Rwanda are examples of the failure of the international community to act decisively to contain conflict. International intervention in the Balkans came only after large numbers of people were displaced. On the other hand, international support for a smooth transition of power in South Africa may have helped to contain and minimize conflict and prevented a refugee problem of huge dimensions.

The second element, preparedness, relates to readiness on the part of UNHCR and other organizations to react quickly to refugee emergencies. This activity is linked to the idea of prevention in that it relies on effective surveillance to determine where crises may occur. An overall refugee response policy requires that organizations concerned with refugees always be ready to respond to situations that would cause people flee their homes.

Because of its extensive experience in managing refugee emergencies, UNHCR is highly prepared to deal with emerging refugee crises. This is also true of other agencies that deal with refugees. However, preparedness is closely related to the ability of these agencies to work in difficult political situations. The ability of these agencies to respond has been hampered sometimes because of the growing reluctance of the major powers to intervene militarily. Preparedness is also challenged by resource constraints. As budgets for refugee relief become more limited, preparedness has been seriously diminished.

The third element, response, concerns the adequacy of the refugee organizations' actions in responding to specific refugee situations. There have been many cases in the past in which international aid agencies have responded chaotically to disasters that involved the displacement of large numbers of people. As a result of these ineffective responses, scarce resources have been squandered, agencies have engaged in unseemly rivalries, logistics have disintegrated, public relations in donor countries has been harmed, and the intended beneficiaries of international aid have suffered. These difficulties have been ameliorated as a result of improved response strategies, but response is still impeded by the lack of support for refugee agencies that work in difficult situations. These agencies have been harassed by armed groups in different parts of the world, their staff members have been intimidated, and supplies have been stolen. The reluctance of the international community to engage in vigorous peacekeeping has compounded the problems facing these organizations.

The fourth element, protection, is a legal concept that seeks to ensure safe passage and security for the refugee populations. The task of ensuring protection is a part of the international mandate of UNHCR. Through use of both its personnel and its influence with governments and the other international agencies, UNHCR seeks to enforce international agreements concerning the safety and security of refugees. This process involves discussions with host governments about the provision of asylum and other services to refugees. It may also involve the use of international peacekeeping forces to safeguard the rights of refugees.

Asylum was once considered sacrosanct, but the climate of receptivity to refugees has cooled in a number of asylum countries. Many people in the host countries have become refugee fatigued and less accommodating. This is particularly true of the industrialized countries. An example of changing attitudes can be seen in Denmark, where laws promulgated a few years ago have made it extremely difficult for asylum seekers to gain entry (Hammer, 1993). These laws are particularly directed at excluding refugees from Africa. Despite the guarantees provided under international refugee law, many more governments now seek to exclude refugees or subtly coerce them into leaving. In recent times countries such as Kenya and Tanzania, apparently under pressure from their electorates, have expressed a reluctance to take in the Rwandan refugees who have flocked to their borders. UNHCR has found itself in the unenviable position of pleading for permission to shelter these refugees. It is sad that this is happening in Africa, which is traditionally renowned for its hospitality to strangers. Although African governments have previously been accommodating to refugees, more African governments are now ambivalent and even hostile toward them (Mupedziswa, 1993).

The fifth element, solution, also gives expression to UNHCR's mandate to respond to the international refugee problem and find durable solutions. The concept of solution is wide ranging, and the response depends on the situation affecting particular refugee groups. It is essentially pragmatic and seeks to formulate solutions based on a realistic assessment of what is possible. In some cases, solution may involve the return of refugees to their homes, but when this is not likely in the long run, it may involve the integration of refugees into the host society. It may also involve resettlement in a third country. However, in all cases, it involves the provision of services to assist refugees in coping with their situation and minimizing the problems they face.

A major problem in providing such services is the increasing scarcity of resources, particularly in developing countries, where social services have been subjected to severe cuts as a result of indebtedness, economic adversity, and the imposition of structural adjustment programs. There are no resources in these countries to provide for refugee populations who stream across national borders. Another problem is the budgetary retrenchment experienced by international agencies. In recent years, UNHCR has experienced financial difficulties that make it difficult for the organization to fulfill its obligations. Budget cuts, and the reported failure of several member countries to meet their financial obligations to the United Nations, make it unlikely that the problem of resources will be resolved in the near future. In 1980 UNHCR was provided with US$60 for each refugee in its care. By 1989 this figure had dropped to US$38 per refugee (Crisp, 1991). In addition, the financial burden of providing services is so great that it cannot be fully assumed by nongovernment organizations.

Another issue is the slowing of voluntary repatriation. Refugees now stay in the host countries for long periods. In some cases it appears unlikely that the refugees will ever return to their homes. It now takes much longer to resolve the conflicts that created the refugee situation. Thus, host countries are obliged to accommodate refugee populations for much longer times, and in many cases, hostility toward refugees has increased, adding to the predicament of asylum seekers.

Also, when it occurs, voluntary repatriation is occurring with growing frequency in conditions of continuing conflict and insecurity, and refugees are returning home without assurances of safety. Often, they return voluntarily only because of the poor conditions in which they live in refugee camps or the hostility of the host society. Much of the blame rests with the host governments, who want refugees to leave as soon as possible. However, some observers have also blamed UNHCR for allowing this trend to continue by not taking a tough line with such governments. On the other hand, there have been successes in securing safe return for some refugees. In 1992 alone about 2.4 million refugees were able to return to their homes (UNHCR, 1993).

Durable solutions to the refugee problem—local integration, resettlement in a third country, and voluntary repatriation—have had a variable effect. Of these three long-term strategies, local integration and settlement in a third country have not worked particularly well. There is a growing belief that both approaches are unrealistic in terms of future directions. Both approaches have benefited only a small fraction of the world's refugee population (Mupedziswa,1993).

Voluntary repatriation to the country of origin is the most favored and realistic policy option for dealing with the refugee problem, particularly in the developing world. However, the adoption of this strategy requires improved conditions in the country of origin, which often is difficult to achieve. For this reason future efforts must focus on preventing emergencies in home countries and emphasizing peacemaking and peacekeeping. UNHCR (1993) contended that governments and international agencies must address the causes of flight before it occurs. This is indeed the direction refugee policy should be taking.

THE ROLE OF SOCIAL WORK IN RESPONDING TO THE REFUGEE PROBLEM

Social workers have an important role to play in addressing the international refugee crisis. They have the requisite knowledge base and skills to work with refugees. As professionals, they understand the interaction between the individual personality and the social environment, so they can provide much-needed counseling services to refugees and at the same time engage in activities that have a wider impact on the welfare of refugees. Social workers are particularly useful in working with vulnerable refugee groups, such as elderly people and abandoned and orphaned children. However, social workers can also transcend their traditional commitments to special-needs groups and play a much more active role in all aspects of refugee assistance (Ahearn, 1995).

Although social workers can make a contribution to the different components of UNHCR's comprehensive refugee policy, they are most likely to be effective when they apply the knowledge, skills, and experiences that are uniquely associated with the profession's historic concerns. Social workers can be involved in prevention, preparedness, response, and, perhaps most extensively, protection and solution, but it is when they apply the interventions for which they are best prepared that they will make the most important difference. In this regard, it is important that social workers be realistic about what they can achieve. Discussions about the involvement of social workers in the field are often excessively ambitious and fail to recognize that social work is only one profession involved in refugee work. For this reason, the following discussion focuses on professional roles that social workers are particularly able to play in the context of refugee assistance, including counseling refugees and their families to cope with personal problems, referring refugees to other sources of assistance, assisting in community organizing with refugee groups, advocating on behalf of refugees, and helping refugee communities engage in developmental activities.

Social work has long been involved in counseling refugees and addressing their psychological problems. As Potocky (1995) pointed out, refugees are in urgent need of mental health services. The traumatic suffering and sense of loss they experience cannot be overemphasized. They have lost families, homes, friends, communities, jobs, and sense of belonging (Ahearn, 1995). Many have been subjected to abuse, physical violence, and deprivation, which leaves long-term psychological scars, especially on the young (McKenzie, Sack, Angell, Manson, & Rath, 1986). In addition to experiencing severe emotional distress, many are mentally ill (Brody,

1994). Along with suffering posttraumatic stress disorder, many have been diagnosed with severe depression and other serious problems (Boehnlein, 1987). There is a great need for effective psychological counseling designed specifically for refugees. The social work literature has begun to discuss the most appropriate forms of refugee counseling (Kelly, 1994; Strober, 1994).

As mental health professionals, social workers can make a significant contribution to the treatment of the emotional and other psychological problems refugees experience. In addition to working in mental health teams that provide conventional counseling services, they have particular skills in providing group treatment to refugees who have experienced similar problems. A good example is group work with refugee women who have been subjected to sexual violence. These highly traumatized women require special assistance that social workers experienced in group activities can provide.

In addition to their role as mental health counselors, social workers can serve as case managers and problem solvers for refugees (Hirayama, Hirayama, & Kuroki, 1995). They are particularly skilled in matching needs and services and can use these skills to bring needed services to refugees. They can also use their knowledge of community resources to refer refugees to appropriate sources of assistance, either with individual refugee clients or for refugee communities. Because of particular skills in working with special-needs groups such as needy children and elderly people, social workers should be given special responsibility for providing services to these groups.

In many countries, refugees live together in close proximity. They may be confined to refugee camps or otherwise gravitate toward each other in particular neighborhoods. Frequently their living conditions are inadequate. Many congregate in squatter communities with limited sanitation, clean water, and other amenities. However, refugees are not helpless, and in most cases, they will organize at the local level to improve their conditions, engage in cooperative activities, and improve their neighborhoods.

Because of social work's special knowledge and long experience in community organization, the profession has an obvious role to play in helping refugee communities improve their environment. Social workers can facilitate and support the local self-help efforts of refugee communities by helping them to obtain access to services and by helping them acquire the assertive, participatory decision-making skills they need to function effectively. As Potocky (1995) argued, social work needs to address empowerment issues and assist refugees to be more effective in securing the services they need. The creation of effective refugee organizations is critical.

Of course, social work can also facilitate the empowerment of refugees by engaging in advocacy and lobbying for them (Ahearn, 1995). Social workers are likely to be most effective when they join with refugee organizations and other politically active groups who seek to promote the interests of refugees. Although it is desirable that all social workers seek to advocate on behalf of refugees, it is likely that organized efforts will be the most successful. For this reason, social work's professional associations should campaign on behalf of refugees.

Where issues of refugee protection and assistance are concerned, social work organizations such as the International Association of Schools of Social Work and the International Federation of Social Workers should take greater advantage of the forums afforded through their observer status at the United Nations. A recent position paper by the National Association of Social Workers in the United States denounced efforts within that country to deny health, housing, and other social services to refugees (Ahearn, 1995). Social workers also need to back efforts to reduce incidences of refugee influxes from occurring in the first instance. Social work associations are most likely to be effective when they seek to deal with political leaders and others in positions of influence at both the national and international levels. In this regard, social work's role in carrying out research and presenting facts on refugee situations should not be overlooked. Social workers have the academic training to engage in research into the needs and circumstances of refugees

Social work should become more involved in development activities with refugees. The developmental perspective in social welfare is now gaining more acceptance in the profession, because social workers appreciate that conventional consumption and maintenance approaches have limited value in dealing with human needs (Midgley, 1995). As resources for refugee services become increasingly strained, the importance of economic self-sufficiency among refugee populations becomes more apparent. It is also now recognized that refugees do not idly wait for services, but they actively engage in economic activities. As UNHCR (1995) reported, research has shown that the notion of refugee dependence is a myth. For example, a group of Ethiopian refugees in Somalia spontaneously engaged in a variety of economic activities to improve their lives. The use of development activities is vital for transforming refugees into assets instead of liabilities (Loescher, 1993).

Social workers can contribute to these activities by, for example, promoting microenterprises, facilitating access to employment, and creating economic cooperatives. As a profession, social work needs to be much more aware of the need for a developmental approach and to be actively involved in activities that will enhance the material welfare of refugees. These activities are needed urgently—not only in refugee camps and settlements, but also when refugees are returned to their homes. When they return to devastated homes and communities, it is critically important that refugees get help to engage in development activities as soon as possible.

CHALLENGES TO SOCIAL WORK

There are great challenges facing social workers in the context of the current global refugee crisis. Unfortunately, the profession has not been very actively involved in contributing to the resolution of this crisis, and it has not demonstrated its willingness to respond to the crisis (Mupedziswa, 1993). Few social workers have been involved in the field and the social work literature on the subject is limited. Despite some discussion of the issue, social work's major professional associations have not organized on behalf of refugees or made effective representation to those in positions of power and influence who are able to bring about improved conditions for refugees.

The profession has not yet developed a specialized body of knowledge related to social work practice with refugees, and there is little curriculum content in social work education dealing with the subject. There is a need for social work to articulate refugee assistance as a substantive field of practice with its own goals, methods, and knowledge base. There is an urgent need to include content about the international refugee crisis in the professional curriculum. Where a curriculum is already in place, it needs to be strengthened.

Social work needs to articulate its role and forcefully demonstrate its potential to help address the global refugee crisis. The millions of desperately needy people among the world's refugees deserve the profession's attention. The crisis is too severe—and the needs of refugees are too great—for social work to neglect this field any longer.

REFERENCES

Ahearn, F. (1995). Displaced people. In R. L. Edwards (Ed.-in-Chief), *Encyclopedia of social work* (19th ed., Vol. 1, pp. 771–780). Washington, DC: NASW Press.

Boehnlein, J. (1987). A review of mental health services for refugees between 1975 and 1985 and a proposal for future services. *Hospital and Community Psychiatry, 38,* 764–768.

Black, R. (1993). Geography and refugees: Current issues. In R. Black & V. Robinson (Eds.), *Geography and refugees* (pp. 3–13). London: Belhaven Press.

Brody, E. (1994). The mental health and well-being of refugees: Issues and directions. In A. Marsella, T. Bornemann, S. Ekblad, & J. Orley (Eds.), *Amidst peril and pain* (pp. 57–68). Washington, DC: American Psychological Association.

Crisp, J. (1991). Refugee protection and assistance: A system in crisis. Unpublished manuscript, Office of the United Nations High Commissioner for Refugees, Geneva.

Hammer, T. (1993). The Sweden-wide strategy of refugee dispersal. In R. Black & V. Robinson (Eds.), *Geography and refugees* (pp. 104–117). London: Belhaven Press.

Hirayama, K., Hirayama, H., & Kuroki, Y. (1995). Southeast Asian refugee resettlements in Japan and the USA. *International Social Work, 38,* 165–176.

Kelly, P. (1994). Integrating systemic and post-systemic approaches to social work practice with refugee families. *Families in Society, 75,* 541–549.

Leopold, M., & Harrell-Bond, B. (1994). An overview of the world refugee crisis. In A. Marsella, T. Bornemann, S. Ekblad, & J. Orley (Eds.), *Amidst peril and pain* (pp. 17–32). Washington, DC: American Psychological Association.

Light, I. (1972). *Ethnic enterprise in America: Business and welfare among Chinese, Japanese and Blacks.* Berkeley: University of California Press.

Loescher, G. (1993). *Beyond charity: International cooperation and the global refugee crisis.* New York: Oxford University Press.

McGregor, J. (1993). Refugees and the environment. In R. Black & V. Robinson (Eds.), *Geography and refugees* (pp. 157–170). London: Belhaven Press.

McKenzie, J. D., Sack, W. H., Angell, R. H., Manson, S., & Rath, B. (1986). The psychiatric effects of massive trauma on Cambodian children: 1. The children. *Journal of the American Academy of Child Psychiatry, 25,* 370–376.

Midgley, J. (1995). *Social development: The developmental perspective in social welfare.* Thousand Oaks, CA: Sage Publications.

Mupedziswa, R. (1993). *Uprooted: Refugees and social work in Africa.* Harare, Zimbabwe: JSDA Publications.

Potocky, M. (1995). Refugee settlement in the United States: Implications for international social welfare. *Journal of Sociology and Social Welfare, 23,* 163–174.

Rogers, R., & Copeland, F. (1993). *Forced migration: Policy issues in the post-Cold War world.* Medford, MA: Tufts University Press.

Sowell, T. (1981). *Ethnic America.* New York: Basic Books.

Strober, S. (1994). Social work interventions to alleviate Cambodian refugee psychological distress. *International Social Work, 37,* 23–35.

United Nations High Commissioner for Refugees. (1993). *The state of the world's refugees: The challenge of protection.* New York: Penguin Books.

United Nations High Commissioner for Refugees. (1995). *The state of the world's refugees: In search of solutions.* Oxford, England: Oxford University Press.

U.S. Committee for Refugees. (1993). *1993 world refugee survey.* Washington, DC: Author.

Widgren, J. (1990). Asylum policy at a turning point. *Refugees, 75,* 22–25.

9

The International AIDS Crisis

Social Work Responses

RONALD J. MANCOSKE

The widespread and worldwide pandemic of HIV and AIDS affects all nations, in differing ways and with differing effects. Outbreaks of new and changing viruses are part of the long history of human survival, although human understanding of viruses is a more recent phenomenon. The hope of containing some illnesses, such as poliomyelitis, has been realized, but other epidemics threaten this hope. HIV and AIDS head the list of newly emerging lethal diseases. In just more than a decade, HIV has been identified and tracked, and treatments have been researched in great detail. Scientific research has transformed AIDS from an unknown, uniformly fatal dreaded killer to a lethal illness with treatments offering potential for containment. The history of this pandemic will be largely influenced by the ways in which the global community interacts with HIV infection.

In less developed nations, AIDS causes a quick death from related illnesses and infections indigenous to the environments. For some people however, AIDS causes a slow, painful death that requires complex and specialized care to which not everyone has access. In more developed countries, with advances in pharmacology and medical treatments on the horizon, AIDS is a complex chronic illness requiring complicated and costly ongoing treatments for those who have access to care. Some people will be able to avoid HIV infection by behavioral, social, and planned community changes. Others, however, will continue to be at risk of infection because of conditions of poverty, ignorance, political instability, desperation, and social traditions.

AIDS is found throughout the world and is no longer limited to small, isolated epidemics. In some sub-Saharan African countries, HIV infection is so entrenched, widespread, and resistant to control that it is endemic—a part of the natural environment. The future course of the AIDS pandemic is a social artifact of a host of forces. How this pandemic plays itself out in human communities will be shaped by actions taken by those communities to influence its course. Human conditions such as poverty, maldistribution of resources, corruption, famine, political instability, migrations, refugee status, and discrimination are pathways that create vulnerability to the spread of HIV. Activities that promote hope, justice, control over one's destiny, economic and social development, and social stability are required to contain HIV throughout the world.

The shape and direction of epidemics are influenced by many forces, including the actions of people. Human suffering fosters vulnerabilities to epidemics, and viral threats exploit human opportunities. Nations that protect their most vulnerable people protect the larger public health. Social workers throughout the world are in an excellent position to promote an understanding of the ways HIV exploits the vulnerable in their countries and of the ways community efforts can affect the course of the pandemic by protecting public health. This focus is a natural fit with the social work traditions of addressing the needs of the most vulnerable (Lee, 1989).

Work with the poor, hungry, uprooted, addicted, and marginalized people in society is the core tradition of social work professionalism. This work toward social justice is the mechanism by which hope of containing HIV infections is created and sustained. This chapter examines the HIV/AIDS pandemic as it has evolved in various nations and then proposes ways in which social workers can respond to the growing global AIDS crisis.

THE HIV PANDEMIC

In late 1995 the World Health Organisation (WHO) estimated that approximately 21 million adults worldwide were living with HIV or AIDS and 7,500 people were newly infected each day (United Nations Global Program on AIDS [UNAIDS], 1996). Of these, about 65 percent, (approximately 13 million people) are from sub-Saharan Africa. About 90 percent of all HIV-positive people live in countries outside Western Europe and North America. WHO has estimated that if the rates follow their projections, by 2000, between 30 million and 40 million adults will have become infected.

Observing the patterns of HIV infection has shown how the virus takes opportunities for spreading, and two important lessons have emerged:

TABLE 9.1 ***ADULT HIV INFECTIONS, 1994***

Region	***Number Infected***	***Prevalence, %***
Africa		
Botswana	125,000	18.0
Kenya	1,000,000	8.3
Nigeria	1,050,000	2.2
Uganda	1,300,000	14.5
Americas		
Bahamas	6,000	3.9
Barbados	4,000	2.8
Brazil	550,000	0.6
Haiti	150,000	4.4
Mexico	200,000	0.4
United States	700,000	0.5
Europe		
Belgium	10,000	0.2
France	90,000	0.3
Italy	90,000	0.3
Spain	120,000	0.6
Switzerland	12,000	0.3
Asia		
India	1,750,000	0.4
Myanmar (Burma)	350,000	1.5
Thailand	700,000	2.1
Australia	11,000	0.1

SOURCE: United Nations Global Program on AIDS (UNAIDS). (1996). *HIV/AIDS epidemic in Africa* (pp. 2–6). New York: Author.

Some approaches lead toward control and containment of the spread of HIV, but other approaches lead toward driving the pandemic underground and away from control. The course of the HIV/AIDS pandemic is directed toward marginalized members of society and those who face discrimination (Balter, 1994). Examples of prevalence of HIV infection in adults in several countries are shown in Table 9.1.

HIV and AIDS in Sub-Saharan Africa

UNAIDS has reported on the devastating impact of HIV on sub-Saharan Africa (1996). Of the 7,500 HIV infections occurring daily in 1996, more than 50 percent occurred in sub-Saharan Africa. More than 50 percent of these infections occurred among women. More than 8 million women in sub-Saharan Africa are infected with HIV. More than 1 million children in Africa are infected as well. In some of the heavily affected areas of sub-Saharan Africa, the rate of new infections is showing signs of slowing and even dropping. However, the overall pandemic continues to show signs of expanding. Garrett (1994) reviewed dozens of epidemiological studies that estimated the global HIV prevalence and found that in some sub-Saharan African nations, up to 40 percent of the women of reproductive age in urban areas were infected with HIV.

Epidemiologic data are not always accurate, however. Predictions are often based on the best available evidence with all its limitations (Samuel & Osmond, 1996). Countries may underestimate HIV prevalence for political and social reasons and also because of a lack of an adequate infrastructure for more precise research on disease prevalence. In the late 1980s official estimates of HIV prevalence in some countries were only 5 percent to 10 percent of WHO estimates (Palca, 1991). No other disease in Africa compares with the public health threat of HIV and AIDS. People from the world's more developed nations have become accustomed to seeing poverty and suffering in Africa to such an extent that they become complacent and apathetic toward more suffering.

The HIV/AIDS pandemic is inextricably linked to social and economic forces that influence public health. Many nations do not face a solitary HIV/AIDS pandemic but a host of epidemics at the same time. Scarce resources are challenged by a variety of health threats such as malaria and tuberculosis, both of which are now showing signs of drug resistance (Garrett, 1994). HIV and AIDS create a vulnerability to other opportunistic infections, which are themselves difficult to diagnose and costly to treat. Medications for controlling infections can cost hundreds of dollars monthly and, in some countries where the average annual income is only in the hundreds of dollars, are out of reach for all but the wealthiest people. The rates of infection vary among countries depending on various factors that promote or impede the spread of HIV. Prevention efforts in some areas help to limit new infections, but risk factors in other areas may rapidly increase infections. For example, in the late 1980s South Africa had few AIDS cases, and those were primarily concentrated among white homosexual and bisexual men. Discriminatory labor policies and racial politics influencing black migrant workers promoted the separation of families and facilitated the spread of the virus by the sex industry. Infection rates grew in conditions of poverty and social disruption. By 1991, in just a few years, more than 400,000 black South Africans were estimated to be infected (Armstrong, 1991).

The increasing rate of deaths attributed to HIV infections is slowing the rate of population growth in some sub-Saharan African nations. The U.S. Bureau of the Census (1994) estimated that in the 16 countries with the highest HIV infection rates, population growth would slow in all countries except Thailand, which is predicted to experience a population decline. The human toll of AIDS was predicted to be 121 million lost lives by 2010 in these 16 countries.

The U.S. Bureau of the Census (1994) also predicted that life expectancies in several countries would plummet as a result of AIDS. For example, in Uganda, life expectancy would have been 59 years without AIDS, but with AIDS the average life expectancy will drop to 32 years by 2010. Approximately 80 percent of deaths in rural Uganda are directly linked to AIDS (Brown, 1993). The only hope of containing this devastation lies with prevention, particularly in the creation of an effective vaccine.

HIV and AIDS in Asia

The initial reactions of some governments in Asia was to downplay the threat of HIV. Some Asian countries initially believed HIV risk was a Western cultural phenomenon and would not affect them (Mancoske, 1985). Many countries began by implementing restrictive policies and legislating testing and control of people infected with HIV, but neither strategy was found to be effective in containing the spread of the virus (Mann, 1992). Intravenous drug abuse, variations in sexual expression, lack of accurate prevention information, drug-resistant diseases, crumbling health care infrastructures, and lack of health care resources have all been risk factors, each taking unique behavioral and social dimensions across various nations. The U.S. Bureau of the Census (1994) estimates that by 2010, Thailand will experience the same losses in population growth and life expectancy and increased child orphan rates, infant mortality, and deaths as is currently experienced in the hardest hit countries of sub-Saharan Africa.

Asia, where the HIV/AIDS pandemic is more recent, could, in the next decade, overtake Africa as the region with the most new infections (Palca, 1991, UNAIDS, 1996). By the end of the 1990s, 42 percent of new HIV infections are predicted to be in Asia, whereas 31 percent of new infections will be in Africa (Tarantala & Mann, 1993). Although India and Thailand account for the current large numbers of HIV infections in Asia, the spread in other countries is imminent. Problems such as co-occurrence with other sexually transmitted diseases (STDs), needle sharing by intravenous drug abusers, the commercial sex industry, and contaminated blood products are driving the rise in HIV infections in many Southeast Asian countries.

HIV and AIDS in Latin America and the Caribbean

Increasing rates of infections are occurring in various Latin American and Caribbean countries, also driven by commercial sex, needle sharing, and high STD rates, as well as by heterosexual transmission—especially by bisexual men and their female partners. It is estimated that, by decade's end, infection rates among intravenous drug users will grow from 20 percent to 60 percent (UNAIDS, 1996). The prevalence of HIV in Brazil and Mexico is similar to the prevalence in Western Europe and the United States.

HIV and AIDS in North America and Western Europe

Infections have largely been clustered among homosexual and bisexual men and among intravenous drug abusers and their sex partners. The latter situation is increasing the rate of heterosexual transmission (UNAIDS, 1996). Holmberg (1996) notes that rates seem to be stabilizing among homosexual men and increasing among intravenous drug users and their sexual partners. The seroprevalence and estimated incidence of HIV infections in the 96 major cities in the United States that were most affected by HIV in 1996 show the rates of HIV infections among special populations (Holmberg, 1996) (see Table 9.2.). HIV and AIDS are increasingly becoming diseases of the poor and marginalized people in the more developed nations, with disproportionately higher rates among ethnic minorities (UNAIDS, 1996). The rates seem to be stabilizing in such Western European countries as Belgium, The Netherlands, Germany, Sweden, and the United Kingdom and increasing in others, such as Spain and Italy.

Poverty among certain segments of the population contributes to the increasing rates of HIV infections among those people most at risk. Problems such as homelessness, barriers to access to care, rapidly increasing STD rates, needle sharing among intravenous drug users, and concentrations of poor and at-risk people in the criminal justice system contribute to this increase. Indices of related public health problems include low vaccination rates among poor people in urban areas, increasing numbers of children living in poverty, an increasing gap between well-off people and poor people, mistrust of government interventions, and retrenchment in

TABLE 9.2 ***ESTIMATED PREVALENCE AND INCIDENCE OF HIV IN 96 MAJOR U.S. CITIES, 1996***

Group at Risk	*Seroprevalence, %*	*Incidence*
Intravenous drug abusers	14.0	1.5/100
Homosexual and bisexual men	18.3	0.7/100
Heterosexual men and women	2.3	0.5/100

SOURCE: Holmberg, S. D. (1996). The estimated prevalence and incidence of HIV in 96 large U.S. metropolitan areas. *American Journal of Public Health, 86*, 642–654.

services to the poor—all have combined to foster pathways for HIV infection. Tuberculosis, a disease believed to have been all but eradicated in the United States 20 years ago is an escalating problem among urban poor people in the United States (McBride, 1991), and it is found increasingly in drug-resistant outbreaks in various countries. Actual rates of tuberculosis are much higher than previous estimates because of inadequate monitoring and outdated treatment models (Garrett, 1994).

HIV and AIDS in Other Parts of the World

HIV infection rates in such areas as North Africa, the Middle East, and Eastern Europe have been low compared with other parts of the world, although evidence indicates that prevalence rates are on the rise in these regions. There are approximately 180,000 HIV infected people in the Middle East (UNAIDS, 1996). Particular factors in creating increased risk are a crumbling health care delivery system; high substance abuse (and intravenous drug use); political instability and conflicts; increasing mobility among populations; and religious fundamentalism, which tends to create outcasts, marginalizes some people, and limits the education and participation of sexual minorities and women.

In an analysis of the HIV epidemic in the former Soviet Union, Williams (1995) outlined a variety of reasons why many of the former Soviet republics are vulnerable to increases in HIV prevalence: coercive testing, stigmatizing risk-group approaches, legislative barriers, emphasis on punitive behavioral controls, high public support for coercive measures, lack of support for risk reduction, and a lack of resources. Some of these countries face dramatic problems with substance abuse, and rates of substance abuse and intravenous drug use appear to be increasing in the 1990s. Life expectancy in Russia is falling, in part because of substance abuse and its related problems (U.S. Bureau of the Census, 1994) and a collapsing health care infrastructure (Williams, 1995). Care and treatment of those ill with HIV disease are often severely limited by a lack of resources.

At-Risk Groups and Behaviors

Despite efforts at HIV prevention that have moved away from discussing at-risk groups and instead talk about at-risk behaviors, some groups remain particularly at risk. Discussions of the risk faced by special population are so sensitive in part because of the history of discrimination and recriminations against those affected. Discrimination includes not just legal oppression but stigmatization, physical attacks on groups perceived to be at risk, imprisonment, quarantines, exacerbated racial conflicts, forced testing, and economic recriminations (Sabatier, 1989).

Most of the people in the world who are infected with HIV are poor. WHO has estimated that 90 percent of the 21 million people infected are from developing countries (UNAIDS, 1996). More than 11 million males and 9 million females are infected with HIV. Women are vulnerable to HIV infection biologically, epidemiologically, and socially. For example, they tend to marry men who are older and who have had more sexual partners, to have less control over use of condoms, and to be financially dependent on men ("Women Infected with the AIDS Virus," 1994). Education works to promote health but is denied many women. In addition, infection has spread because women have been subjected to widespread rape in countries at war. In general, women's inequality, which is imposed by cultural, religious, and economic circumstances, enhances their risk for HIV infections.

Youths are particularly vulnerable to HIV infection. Half of all infections so far have been among people between 15 and 24 years old. In some countries, 60 percent of all infections are among youths, with female-to-male ratios of 2 to 1 (UNAIDS, 1996). The popular belief that sex education may encourage sexual activity among youths is a powerful barrier to protection from HIV infection despite evidence to the contrary. Sex education tends in fact, to delay the onset of sexual activity ("Women Infected," 1994).

In the United States, one-quarter of all new HIV infections occurs in youths. This means two people in the United States become infected every hour of every day (Office of National AIDS Policy, 1996). Worldwide, about 1.5 million children (infants and children younger than 15 years of age) have been infected with HIV. Half of them have developed AIDS and almost 5 million children have been orphaned by AIDS (UNAIDS, 1996).

IMPACTS OF THE HIV/AIDS PANDEMIC

Because HIV and AIDS have disproportionate impacts on people in the most productive period of their lives, the effect of the pandemic on the economic structures of nations is felt more directly than the effects of other illnesses that cause disability at later stages of life. Armstrong (1992) outlined areas of economic impact caused by HIV. The direct costs of medical care, morbidity and mortality, and economic well-being are all directly affected. In some sub-Saharan African areas, where up to 75 percent of hospital beds are occupied by people with HIV-related disease, treatment resources have been drained. By 2015 an estimated 78 percent of all deaths in Burundi and Uganda will be AIDS related ("Africa Will Suffer," 1991). The cost of medical care requires shifting resources away from other health care needs and away from economic development. Countries have to choose between spending on economic and social development and the increasing demands from the health care sector. Even in richer nations, proposals for the rationing of health care have become more frequent as growing percentages of resources are directed toward health care. New evidence shows that specialty care in HIV services contributes to increased survival (Kitahata et al., 1996). This requires increasing investment in the training of health care providers.

Youths who are greatly affected by the HIV/AIDS pandemic include those with valuable job skills that are needed to advance economic development. Key industries, including tourism in some countries, have been particularly hard hit. Some countries have been reluctant to report HIV infection for fear of frightening away tourists. Some have even undercounted HIV infections to minimize the loss of tourist dollars (Palca, 1991). Countries that rely on foreign trade and investments from foreign capital have been fearful of how investors would view them if HIV infection rates increased. Foreign investments could be curtailed as investors identify countries as being at high risk because of the economic impact of HIV and AIDS. Some countries may have to replace skilled, educated workers with expensive foreign laborers.

Armstrong (1992) also has outlined the ways in which agriculture has been affected by HIV and AIDS. Countries where a greater proportion of the national energy is devoted to food production and that also have high HIV prevalence will face difficulties in ensuring adequate agricultural labor supplies. In areas where up to 20 percent of the population is infected with HIV, such as in the less developed countries of central Africa, young laborers will be in short supply, limiting the production and distribution of food. Costs of products will increase as stockpiles of supplies decrease in areas where greater portions of income already are devoted to food production and supply. When crops are sold on international markets in these circumstances, foreign exchange ratios are threatened.

Barriers to agricultural production in less developed nations also increase the vulnerability to the spread of HIV (Armstrong, 1992). Families living on the edge of malnutrition are pushed into desperation when young adults die, leaving both older and younger family members responsible for food production. The impact of HIV and AIDS at the most productive ages weakens families. Illness creates greater poverty, which in time forces family members into migration, the sex industry, or other circumstances that destabilize family life. These circumstances contribute to agricultural practices that focus on quick, short-term returns rather than long-term and more ecologically beneficial practices. Subsistence living does not allow for ecologically sound agricultural practices.

The United Nations Food and Agriculture Organization has estimated that in Africa, the overall agricultural labor force—predominantly women—will be reduced by 25 percent by 2010 because of HIV (Garrett, 1994). People in their most productive years are lost to illness and death, some of them with skills and education that offer hope for future social and economic development.

Just as some U.S. inner-cities appear to be crumbling under the weight of the problems of the urban underclass, in some rural agrarian countries, health is crumbling under the weight of poverty. Cultural and legal constrictions give many women little alternative but to turn to the sex industry for economic survival. This in turn further promotes the spread of HIV infection.

Impact on Families

Families are often financially devastated by HIV and AIDS. Financial loss includes the direct costs of care and treatment, lost time, and lost productivity. Time at work and other activities that support families are lost. Other costs can include medication, hospitalization, other treatment, transportation to health care centers, and finally, funeral expenses.

Extended families provide resources for care. Ell and Northen (1990) estimated that 80 percent of the care of sick people in the United States is provided by family members. The potential for care by extended families is an asset of tremendous social, psychological, and financial benefit, but these families need support such as resources, referral networks, and social services. More than half the orphans in Uganda are now cared for by extended families (UNAIDS, 1996), and by 2015 there will be an estimated 16 million orphans in Africa ("Africa Will Suffer," 1991). In some cases, grandparents are caring for as many as 15 grandchildren left orphaned by the deaths of their parents. About 30 to 40 percent of these children are also HIV infected (UNAIDS, 1966).

When large numbers of the middle generation are sick or dying, resources are devoted to caring for the ill, reducing access to other things that families need. Progress made by women in improving educational opportunities may be lost when time and resources are needed to care for the ill. When young parents become ill, children are directly affected by the decreased earning capacity and restricted opportunities of the parents. Women traditionally are the first to have to stay home and help with caregiving.

Women may be the most vulnerable to the impact of HIV and AIDS, whether they become ill or are the survivors. In all societies, women are primary providers of child care, often with economic help from men. In some developing countries, when a women loses her husband, she is forced to take on the combined burden of child care, family support, food production, and care of family members. When women are free to move in and about in the economic activities of the country, these burdens are a less onerous challenge than in those countries where women's economic equality is restricted by law, custom, education, and religious beliefs. If all things were equal, women and men would bear similar burdens as survivors. However, all things are not equal for women in many circumstances, and being a survivor brings them new burdens and inequities.

Children in areas with high HIV and AIDS rates are particularly vulnerable to the ravages of HIV. The U.S. Bureau of the Census (1994) estimated that in several of the high-prevalence areas of Africa, approximately 15 percent of the children have been orphaned by AIDS. The future forebodes similar tragedies for several Asian countries in the next wave of high HIV prevalence. New policies and social services are needed for those who take care of children left behind.

Medical Care and HIV/AIDS Treatment

There are differing circumstances in the world of AIDS care. In the United States, with its patchwork health care system, some people with AIDS will receive new medications—others without health insurance will not receive state-of-the-science treatments. After years of research and development, few drugs are available for AIDS treatment, and they are very expensive. As AIDS activist Larry Kramer (1996) noted, finally there are drugs that may allow people to live longer—but few can afford them. This is also the case in many developing nations.

Home-based care for HIV-related disease is essential to prevent overcrowded hospitals from limiting the care of people with other diseases because of high costs. For example, 7 percent of Malawi's health care budget is AIDS related, as is 9 percent of Rwanda's, 10 percent of Burundi's, and 55 percent of Uganda's (Garrett, 1994).

The varying mechanisms countries use to deliver health care services mean that costs vary greatly, and estimates of costs of lifetime care of HIV-related diseases also vary greatly. In the United States, considerable efforts are devoted to cost containment by various funding and services delivery mechanisms. Costs estimates change as medical treatments shift: More effective treatments mean that people are living longer and are more successfully surviving opportunistic infections as a result of aggressive treatments. Estimates of the cost of individual care in the United States vary from less than $20,000 to more than $200,000 annually (Scitovsky, 1988). Kramer (1996) noted that basic prophylactic treatments for people who do not have opportunistic infections cost approximately $19,000—and this is without taking into account the new protease inhibitors, which add another $6,000 to $8,000 a year. Costs of treating AIDS-related opportunistic infections in the United States average $50,000 per person for medications (Kramer, 1996).

In some African nations, annual treatment costs including medications are limited to $600 to $800 (Over, Bertozzi, & Chin, 1988). Even at an average cost of $600 per person, the treatment of approximately 1 million infected people means an annual cost of $600 million for minimal care. Most developing countries cannot spend that amount. Poor countries without resources for health care in general have neither the capacity nor the primary care infrastructure to treat HIV and AIDS prophylactically, aggressively, or, in many cases, even palliatively.

Many countries have few resources to devote to health care services, and health care infrastructures are limited in what they can offer, even for public health threats. For example, Williams (1995) reported that a quarter of Russian hospitals lack sewer connections, one-fifth are without central heating, and half do not have shower facilities—some do not even have running water. Chronic shortages of clean hypodermic syringes make most infection control practices difficult. Staff, drugs, and equipment are in short supply. Both staff and patients are jeopardized by infections of all kinds because routine medical care procedures are unavailable.

Increased risk of new infections is exacerbated by methods of health care services delivery. Reports of health care workers reusing hypodermic syringes are not uncommon in developing countries. Shortages of syringes, as well as of disinfectants, latex gloves, clean water, and electricity, increase the risk of HIV infection in health care delivery settings. In 1993 people in developing countries died twice as fast from HIV-related infections as those in western countries. (Brown, 1993). Those gaps widen as medical technology available in developed countries improves.

Policies and legislation characterized by repression, xenophobia, and power in the hands of a few also are forces in health care delivery that foster the spread of HIV (Sills, 1994). Just as there are many factors that enhance risk, there are multiple interactive forces that impede health care delivery.

SOCIAL WORK RESPONSES TO THE HIV/AIDS CRISIS

As the global impact of HIV and AIDS expands, social workers are responding in many areas of practice and agency settings. However, social workers often express a reluctance to work in the area of HIV and AIDS (NASW, 1995) and social work educators are often reluctant to teach specifically about the pandemic (Steiner, 1995). The HIV/AIDS pandemic is a biological, psychological, and social phenomenon. A community approach to confronting it requires the active involvement of affected families, as well as the involvement of agencies that provide health and social services. Social work needs to creatively and actively join families and health care services in interdisciplinary efforts to confront the challenges posed by HIV and AIDS.

With nearly two decades of experience with AIDS, broadly defined social developmental approaches have been shown to be effective in controlling the further spread of HIV. Various methods are now commonly known, including avoidance of contaminated blood products and control of blood supplies; safer sex practices that emphasize abstinence, fidelity, and condom use; early and effective care; and human rights of people with HIV and AIDS (Merson, 1995). Midgley (1996a) noted three key areas in which social work contributes to social development: mobilizing resources, organizing communities to promote development, and helping vulnerable populations become more productive. Social workers are already actively involved in many of these functions, but more involvement is needed.

The HIV/AIDS pandemic takes on different proportions and causes different effects in various countries. All countries with low HIV prevalence will not become high-prevalence countries, but they do face the potential of increased HIV prevalence. Although socially created vulnerabilities increase risk of the spread of HIV, there are wide-ranging educational, economic, public health, and social development opportunities to successfully reduce the growth of the prevalence of HIV infections. Social workers can play an important role in these efforts because of their involvement in a variety of services to vulnerable populations.

Dubos (1980) said that the two most critical threats to health are malnutrition and infection, and the best way to combat these threats is to adopt health measures that successfully and simultaneously confront them. Thus, public health planning includes social planning. Successful HIV/AIDS prevention programs are concerned with the protection of human rights, are well managed, have adequate resources, and are based in community actions (UNAIDS, 1996). This approach ensures successful social services programs. Social work should be actively involved in public health activities, community-based organizations, and advocacy efforts in HIV/AIDS prevention.

Social Work in Health Care Services

The systems for the delivery of health care services are complex. Social work often plays an ancillary role in many of these systems, but social workers may provide administrative, organizing, planning, and research support for health care services. Social work responses to HIV and AIDS need to cover the continuum of care: prevention, research, treatment, and bereavement services.

Social work in health care traditionally provides individual, family, and small-group interventions to address individual supports and treatment and social change needs. Preferred models of social work assessment and ensuing interventions emphasize strengths and self-affirmations and move away from medical diagnostic models that have tended to overemphasize pathology and deficits. This emphasis in the counseling process on strengths contributes to the promotion of self-care, healthy adaptation, and learning from adversities to promote broader psychosocial wellness (Mancoske & Lindhorst, 1995). Individual social services address the particular needs of suffering people and effectively bring together community care resources to promote community vitality.

Family practice in social work is often the preferred form of providing direct services because it builds on the strengths of systems that reinforce change and promote adaptation. Generally, families are not only care providers but also advocates for the people who are ill, as well as for resources and for changing health care delivery systems. Families are integral to consumer participation and care coordination. Some people argue for the status quo—for example, arguing that condom use is in violation of cultural or religious norms—and families may be best able to counteract this regressive approach with common-sense public health promotion. Social work traditions encourage the use of family strengths to mobilize people who are suffering to provide leadership in confronting problems beyond individual need.

Group work also starts at the individual level of suffering and moves people to confront suffering at the community level. It challenges the individualizing of suffering and is useful to health care services in both prevention and treatment. The self-help focus is useful not only in confronting the many psychosocial problems of individuals at risk but also as a mechanism for empowering group members to recognize difficulties in their lives and to develop the means to challenge threats to their lives and those of their loved ones (Mancoske & Lindhorst, 1994). This empowering approach in social work practice facilitates problem solving and enhances approaches to care that emphasize not defeatism but the power of moving toward a common good. Group work offers the potential to move beyond psychological education into action to promote well-being. It also helps to overcome the impediments of traditional thinking about new threats to health and well-being. Individual healing is noble—group mobilization is regenerative.

Social Work in Community-Based Care

Social workers serve in many nongovernment, community-based organizations. Nongovernment organizations have been particularly successful in early response to disease threats because they emerge quickly, reach people widely, and frequently side with oppressed people in human rights issues (Tarantala & Mann, 1993). Social workers in these organizations can build on the strengths of communities in confronting HIV risk, and they often provide leadership and support for the development of local community programs.

Community-based services agencies are generally decentralized, coordinated with local leadership and linked to existing community concerns. These agencies rapidly respond to emerging needs among the most vulnerable populations. Such early interventions have occurred in a variety of nations in the response to the HIV/AIDS pandemic. Community-based

HIV/AIDS prevention and control programs built into existing services are found in educational programs, harm reduction programs for problems associated with sex and drugs, programs for control of co-occurring contagious disease epidemics (including tuberculosis, malaria, and STDs), and community-based health care delivery systems that focus on special populations (Anderson & May, 1992).

Social workers in existing community-based service systems can help promote community leadership in the response to HIV and AIDS. It is effective to support local community leadership (Van Gorder, 1995). It is also part of traditional social work practice from an empowerment perspective, which strengthens vulnerable people to promote their own self-care and protection (Dicks, 1994). Coalition-building activities provide opportunities to share expertise as community-based organizations provide leadership for diverse groups to work together on common health promotion activities. Social workers help develop technical expertise and shared resources for work among diverse yet vulnerable populations, such as sex industry workers; gay, lesbian, bisexual, and transgendered people; women; and drug users. Mobilization of these groups helps build constituencies and empower marginalized populations for mutual protection.

Social workers can promote the development of community-based organizations by conducting fundraising around the interests of special populations, such as development of support from international communities for activities based on mutual interests. Some programs receive support from other nations, from churches, from international gay and lesbian human rights interests, from ethnic-based interest groups, and from women's groups.

The effectiveness of an HIV/AIDS prevention program is enhanced when local and national media are used effectively. Social workers who work with populations at risk or in health services can use the media to promote risk reduction and prevention of infection. HIV/AIDS prevention can be successfully publicized to promote the common good without inviting backlash from religious or cultural groups. People learn best when the messages are significant, culturally sensitive, targeted to specific groups, well focused, and designed to evoke positive responses. Such messages are best delivered by people with whom the public can identify. Community-based organizations that have earned public support can best promote these messages.

HIV and AIDS information from social workers delivering services in relevant community-based organizations is often more trusted than messages from anonymous, abstract, or distant sources, including government sources. Agencies that provide services in other health-related areas can develop a targeted and focused message as an effective way of reaching people at risk. Effective media campaigns have reduced the spread of HIV in various countries (Mann, 1992). It is necessary to evaluate health promotion efforts to ensure that the most significant messages reach the right audience, messages are not contradictory or too vague to understand, and they do not overlap for some populations and miss others. Effective use of peers in promoting education and behavior change also influences successful media programming.

Social Work Advocacy

In many countries social workers are actively involved in care for particularly vulnerable populations. For example, social workers are actively involved in care and services for people with mental illness, substance abuse problems, refugees, sexual minorities, and the poorest people in those countries. These activities provide access to those most vulnerable to HIV-infection risk.

The commitment to human rights in the United Nations Charter provides a key element in how best to respond to HIV and AIDS. In many countries HIV infection and AIDS are conditions of poor and marginalized people. Social workers can promote access to care, nondiscrimination, social assistance, and cooperation. Bringing information about HIV and AIDS to social work clients and providing accessible resources, in culturally acceptable ways, is the way to successful HIV and AIDS prevention and to health promotion.

Social workers are involved in the promotion of human rights. In some countries, such as in the former Soviet Union, public opinion generally favors restrictions on human rights in a response to HIV and AIDS (Williams, 1995). Through community activities, educational programs, and community organizing, social workers can educate the public on the limitations of restrictive approaches in HIV control. The more the public feels vulnerable, the more likely are restrictive measures to be applied, despite evidence that this approach does not work (Mann, 1992). Although social workers are involved in educating the community about HIV and AIDS risk, they also need to educate people about how to effectively prevent the illness in their communities without irrational discrimination against the people who are already infected.

Social workers can be integral in advocacy efforts to promote funding for prevention and care of HIV-related illnesses. Resources for appropriate care and treatment are not available to poor people in most countries of the world. Although the industrialized world has less than 25 percent of the world's population, about 18 percent of AIDS cases, and 15 percent of new HIV infections yearly, it accounts for 95 percent of the resources spent on AIDS care (Tarantala & Mann, 1993). Survival is based on the quality of care available. Social workers should be informed of best practices and standards of care and ways to promote access to services for everyone who needs them in every country.

Providing care to those affected by HIV and AIDS is not the sole responsibility of any particular group. Care is most effective when support is provided not only for those infected, but also for caregivers and others whose lives are affected by a person's illness, whether they are health and social services providers, partners, families, or supportive communities. Efforts to promote supports for all involved, including caregivers, empower the care delivery network and minimize the risk of burnout. Services to caregivers allow them to remain actively involved even while they are contending with their own worries, fears, and grief (Walker, Pomeroy, McNeil, & Franklin, 1996).

Social workers involved in public efforts to promote stability and peace can incorporate HIV and AIDS prevention into their working agendas. Policies that promote political stability and participation work to empower citizenry. The need to promote participation by those affected by HIV and AIDS must, however, be balanced with confidentiality.

Social workers are especially capable of working with special populations, such as prisoners, sex industry workers, ethnic minority communities, asylum seekers, sexual minorities, intravenous drug abusers, refugees, or other marginalized groups. When policies or legislation to restrict human rights are promoted, political advocacy is necessary. Social workers in HIV and AIDS services have been successful in advocacy approaches to reach community-based health and social services providers, communities, and the public.

There is a need to emphasize the primacy of nondiscrimination, encourage international cooperation rather than restrictiveness, and promote development of resources for the health and social services infrastructures. These activities fit with the social work practice model that emphasizes social development over treatment approaches (Ngan & Hui, 1996).

Social workers often can affect delivery of HIV and AIDS care services to the marginalized people in their countries. For example, intravenous drug abusers are often clients, whether in treatment, criminal justice settings, health care services, or family work. Social workers can help control the rise of HIV infection by including needle exchange programs in their services systems. Needle exchange programs are often politically unpopular, although evidence of their effectiveness in reducing HIV transmission is strong, as well as evidence that they do not encourage drug use (National Commission on AIDS, 1991). Laws against over-the-counter needle sales limit supplies, encourage needle sharing, and increase the risk of HIV infection. When alcohol, drug, or other mental health treatment is weak, risk of HIV infection is increased. Social workers need to identify barriers and advocate for effective interventions.

Untreated STDs also increase the risk of HIV infection by 300 percent to 400 percent (UNAIDS, 1996). Successful STD control programs include promoting safer sex behaviors. For example, early diagnosis and treatment programs in Tanzania in the early 1990s brought about a 42 percent decrease in new STD infections (UNAIDS, 1996).

In some countries HIV infection may reach saturation (the point where all of those most vulnerable to infection become infected), but widespread prevalence can be contained before the saturation point if communities respond effectively ("AIDS—Displaying the Global Dynamics," 1994). Social workers can be at the forefront of this effort if they adhere to their traditions and maintain activities that promote justice and, hence, health. HIV is a given in nature, but HIV prevalence is a social artifact. The promotion of public health is the promotion of conditions in which people can be healthy (Institute of Medicine, 1988). Social workers and public health and community groups must be persistent if their work for health promotion can have an impact. When communities and nations fail to successfully control HIV and AIDS, suffering is widespread. Affected communities must be empowered to be actively involved (Van Gorder, 1995). Social work models that emphasize social development (Midgley, 1996b) offer ways for social work to have an impact on public health, social development, and the needs of individuals in harm's way of not only poverty and inequality but also the HIV/AIDS pandemic.

REFERENCES

Africa will suffer "millions" of AIDS orphans. (1991). *New Scientist, 129,* 123.

AIDS—Displaying the global dynamics [Editorial]. (1994). *American Journal of Public Health, 84,* 175.

Anderson, R. M., & May, R. M. (1992). Understanding the AIDS pandemic. *Scientific American, 266*(5), 58–66.

Armstrong, J. (1991). South Africa and the threat of AIDS. *New Scientist, 129,* 136.

Armstrong, J. (1992). The demographic, economic, and social impact of AIDS. In J. M. Mann (Ed.), *AIDS in the world* (pp. 195–226). Cambridge, MA: Harvard University Press.

Balter, M. (1994). UN readies a new global AIDS program. *Science, 266,* 1312–1313.

Brown, P. (1993). Uganda AIDS. *New Scientist, 138,* 6.

Dicks, B. A. (1994). African-American women and AIDS: A public health and social work challenge. *Social Work in Health Care, 19*(3/4), 123–143.

Dubos, R. (1980). *Man adapting.* New Haven, CT: Yale University Press.

Ell, K., & Northen, H. (1990). *Families and health care: Psychosocial practice.* New York: Aldine de Gruyter.

Garrett, L. (1994). *The coming plague: Newly emerging diseases in a world out of balance.* New York: Penguin Books.

Holmberg, S. D. (1996). The estimated prevalence and incidence of HIV in 96 large US metropolitan areas. *American Journal of Public Health, 86,* 642–654.

Institute of Medicine. (1988). *The future of public health.* Washington, DC: National Academy Press.

Kitahata, M. M., Koepsell, T. D., Deyo, R. A., Maxwell, C. L., Dodge, W. T., & Wagner, E. H. (1996). Physicians' experience with AIDS as a factor in survival. *New England Journal of Medicine, 334*(11), 701–706.

Kramer, L. (1996, July 14). A good news/bad news AIDS joke. *New York Times Magazine,* pp. 26–29.

Lee, J. (1989). *Group work with the poor and the oppressed.* New York: Haworth Press.

Mancoske, R. (1985). Social services with the terminally ill: AIDS crisis in Hong Kong. *Hong Kong Journal of Social Work, 19*(1), 17–21.

Mancoske, R. J., & Lindhorst, T. (1994). Group work practice in an HIV outpatient clinic. In M. Campbell (Ed.), *Group work in the 1990's* (pp. 71–81). New Orleans: Tulane University Press.

Mancoske, R. J., & Lindhorst, T. (1995). The ecological context of HIV counseling. In G. A. Lloyd & M. A. Kuszelewicz (Eds.), *HIV disease* (pp. 25–41). New York: Haworth Press.

Mann, J. M. (1992). AIDS and human rights. In J. M. Mann (Ed.), *AIDS in the world* (pp. 537–573). Cambridge, MA: Harvard University Press.

McBride, D. (1991). *From TB to AIDS: Epidemics among urban blacks since 1900.* Albany: State University of New York Press.

Merson, M. (1995). AIDS: What can be done. *UNESCO Courier, 48,* 10–13.

Midgley, J. (1996a). Involving social workers in economic development. *International Social Work, 39,* 13–25.

Midgley, J. (1996b). Towards a developmental model of social policy: Relevance of the Third World experience. *Journal of Sociology and Social Welfare, 23*(1), 59–74.

National Association of Social Workers, Task Force on HIV/AIDS. (1995). *Assessing social workers' responses to HIV/AIDS.* Washington, DC: Author.

National Commission on AIDS. (1991). *America living with AIDS.* Washington DC: Author.

Ngan, R., & Hui, S. (1996). Economic and social development in Hong Kong and southern China: Implications for social work. *International Social Work, 39,* 83–95.

Office of National AIDS Policy. (1996). *Youth and HIV/AIDS: An American agenda.* Washington DC: Author.

Over, M., Bertozzi, S., & Chin, J. (1988, June). The direct and indirect cost of HIV infections in developing countries. Paper presented at the 4th International AIDS Conference, Stockholm.

Palca, J. (1991). The sobering geography of AIDS. *Science, 252,* 372–373.

Sabatier, R. (1989). *AIDS and the third world.* Santa Cruz, CA: New Society.

Samuel, M. C., & Osmond, D. E. (1996). Uncertainties in the estimation of HIV prevalence and incidence in the United States. *American Journal of Public Health, 86,* 627–628.

Scitovsky, A. (1988). The economic impact of AIDS in the United States. *Health Affairs, 7*(3), 1–14.

Sills, Y. G. (1994). *The AIDS pandemic: Sociological perspectives.* Westport, CT: Greenwood Press.

Steiner, S. J. (1995). Understanding HIV and AIDS: Preparing students for practice. *Journal of Social Work Education, 31,* 322–336.

Tarantala, D., & Mann, J. (1993). Coming to terms with the AIDS pandemic. *Issues in Science and Technology, 9*(3), 41–48.

United Nations Global Program on AIDS. (1996, March). *HIV/AIDS epidemic in Africa.* New York: Author. (http://www.who.ch/gpahome.htm).

U.S. Bureau of the Census. (1994). *World population profile: 1994.* New York: Gordon Press.

Van Gorder, D. (1995). Building community and cultural care essential to successful HIV prevention among gay and bisexual men. *AIDS Public Policy Journal, 10*(2), 65–74.

Walker, R. J., Pomeroy, E. C., McNeil, J. S., & Franklin, C. (1996). Anticipatory grief and AIDS: Strategies for intervening with caregivers. *Health & Social Work, 21,* 49–57.

Williams, C. (1995). *AIDS in post-communist Russia and its successor states.* Brookfield, VT: Ashgate.

Women infected with the AIDS virus [Editorial]. (1994). *Futurist, 28*(2), 62–63.

10

Social Work as an International Profession

Opportunities and Challenges

TOM JOHANNESEN

A listing of milestones in the development of social work and social welfare through history starts with King Hammurabi in Babylon. He issued his Code of Justice in 1750 BCE, which included a requirement that people help one another during times of hardship (Barker, 1995). More modern is Mary E. Richmond's book, *Friendly Visiting among the Poor* (1899/1969). The year after its publication, she had a dispute with educator Simon N. Patten (who coined the term "social workers") about whether social workers' major role should be advocacy or delivering individualized social services. Later discussions during this century centered on whether social work is a profession or semiprofession (Hugman, 1996).

As a new century approaches, what are the challenges and opportunities for the social work profession from an international perspective? This chapter focuses on the role of the International Federation of Social Workers (IFSW) and its perspective on the agenda for the development of social work in the years ahead, and on the United Nations (UN) as a major initiator of international cooperation and programs for social development.

GLOBAL TRENDS SHAPING OUR FUTURE

The world at the end of this millennium is marked by a globalization process gaining momentum from day to day. The village formed the framework in which most people experienced their environment in the days of our grandparents. Later the reference point expanded—first to the nation, then to the region, and now to the entire globe. Today we are more dependent on each other than ever before. Globalization is a consequence of increased human mobility, enhanced communications, greatly increased trade and capital flows, and technological developments. In turn it has created opportunities for growth and development and permitted countries to share experiences and learn from each other. It also promotes a cross-fertilization of ideals, cultural values, and aspirations (UN, 1995). Still, only certain segments of the population benefit from globalization. It helps some people develop their international links, their understanding of others, and their communication skills. At the same time, others—and in many countries the majority of the population—are left behind in intensified poverty, unemployment, and social disintegration.

The explosion of education is another powerful force shaping the future. Never before have so many people been so well educated—and never before have so many entered universities and then continued to educate themselves throughout their lives. The 13 countries with the highest number of years of schooling average 11 years or more (*The Economist,* 1995). However, many other people throughout the world are left behind, without access to education that can lead to skilled work later in life. Education plays a key role in bringing a country from poverty to prosperity, as has been demonstrated by the so-called East Asian "tigers" (Hong Kong, Korea, Taiwan, and Singapore). Failure to invest in education of young people generates other costs for society. Those who are poorly educated make up a large proportion of people who are unemployed and living in poverty, consuming a disproportionate share of public services and expenditures (Barr, 1994).

Although it takes various forms, the market approach to the economy is now, globally, almost the sole approach. Reduction of public expenditures is often part of what is called the free-market philosophy. In countries in political, economic, and social transition, this experience has been difficult for large parts of the population. Even if the overall objectives of the reforms are to achieve higher living standards and greater individual freedom (Barr, 1994), the structural adjustments recommended by some to reach this goal cause considerable pain. Kramer (1995, p. 5) describes this process for Europe in a lively way: "The pace of social and economic change in Europe has suddenly accelerated from a leisurely jog to a sprint."

Some negative results of change are exemplified in Russia, where the number of people in poverty increased from 12 percent of the population in 1990 to 37 percent in 1992. The figures are even more striking for Russian families with three children or more. In this group 72 percent were registered as poor in the first quarter of 1993 (Barr, 1994). Another country marked by structural adjustment programs is Zimbabwe, where fees for public education were introduced as a result of a direct demand from the International Monetary Fund. In one area of Harare, the capital, half of the households have to go to the social welfare office to try to obtain a share of the very limited resources available to pay tuition. In Morocco, public hospitals now charge for services, and the decay of public schools has led to the emergence of private schools with high fees, which are beyond the reach of the majority of the population (UN, 1994).

THE UNITED NATIONS WORLD SUMMIT: COMMITMENTS FROM WORLD LEADERS AND CHALLENGES FOR SOCIAL WORKERS

The United Nations World Summit for Social Development held in Copenhagen in March 1995 was one in a series of landmark world conferences organized by the UN in the 1990s. It marked the first time in history that world leaders came together to focus on policies and programs to address global social problems. The three main themes of the summit were eradicating poverty, fighting unemployment, and fostering social integration.

This social summit produced a declaration and a program of action to bring the world forward. The declaration contains 10 commitments within a framework of international cooperation but with full respect for national sovereignty (UN, 1995, pp. 12–33):

- creation of an enabling environment
- eradication of poverty
- full employment
- social integration
- equality and equity between women and men
- access to quality education and health
- accelerated economic, social and human resource development in Africa
- ensuring that structural adjustment programs (SAPs) include social development goals
- increasing and/or using more effectively resources allocated to social development

- improving the framework for international, regional, and subregional cooperation for social development.

Implementation of these commitments would change the world.

The themes and commitments of the social summit offer both opportunities for and challenges to international social work. Social workers in different parts of the world daily meet the challenges of poverty, unemployment, and social exclusion. Upgrading the importance of social issues on the global agenda is possible only if there is a movement from awareness to action—internationally, nationally, and locally. With its potential to help bring about change, professional social work is positioned to be a major contributor to the implementation process (IFSW, 1995).

Eradicating Poverty

Poverty is a concept that connotes a lack of acceptable living standards. It may refer to absolute poverty, which is human deprivation at its most extreme, or relative poverty, in which individuals or groups live on one-half or less of a nation's median income. Poverty is generally characterized by lack of sufficient income to purchase basic necessities of life such as health care, education, housing, transportation, clothing, and food (Hall, 1995).

Worldwide, one in every five people—more than 1.5 billion—lives below the poverty line (United Nations Department of Public Information [UNDPI], 1995). Today this number is increasing by 25 million people per year. Twenty percent of the world's population survive on a daily income of less than one U.S. dollar. In the poorest 15 countries of the world, the gross domestic product (GDP) per person is US$200 or less per year, yet the 15 richest countries have GDPs over US$21,000 per person per year. The life expectancy in Sierra Leone is 41 years, but it is 80 in Japan. Kenya has more than 70,000 people per doctor, and Italy has 210 (*The Economist,* 1996). A UN estimate shows that fewer than 10 percent of the world's total population participate fully in the political, economic, social, and cultural institutions that shape their lives (UNDPI, 1994). Women, elderly people, children, disabled people, members of minority groups, and those who dwell in rural areas are the most marginalized.

Poverty has been a main area of concern for professional social work since its beginning. Over the years social work's role in addressing this concern has been transformed from a remedial welfare function to an approach more oriented toward development. Social workers now aim to mobilize resources and opportunities to assist those disadvantaged by the system to help themselves as much as possible. This is conceptualized as social development, as explained in Hall (1995, p. 155):

> Social development emphasizes both the need for more comprehensive and coordinated policy and planning on a regional and national basis, and the need to help indigenous groups to organize in order to influence political and bureaucratic structures to more completely address their particular needs.

Hall (1995) pointed out that there are a number of strategies social workers can use as part of a development approach to human welfare. One set of strategies is directed at providing income-earning opportunities for poor people. These strategies include promoting employment creation through neighborhood or local community investment, advocating for access to credit for investment, and encouraging the establishment of small, productive enterprises that are growth oriented and labor intensive. A related strategy is political action to produce more equitable distribution of land and prosocial use of government funds. Political action should also be directed at limiting restrictive regulations that inhibit the operation of local informal economic activities, such as vending foodstuffs or trading goods through a barter system. Such action requires the use of mass media to create greater public awareness of poverty and its effects.

Fighting Unemployment

Productive work and employment are central elements of development as well as decisive elements of human identity (UN, 1995). Still, unemployment and underemployment are growing in many countries of the world. This fact is linked to the basic challenge facing the international economy: the interrelation between a free-market economy and sustainable social development. The level of political maturity in the world to deal with this interrelation in an effective way does not yet exist. After the collapse of most socialist systems, the free-market economy is the ideological winner of the Cold War. However, global society has yet to balance economic freedom with full employment politics. In fact, the SAPs promoted by the World Bank and the International Monetary Fund and adopted by many governments have increased the problem of unemployment.

One of the main achievements of the social summit was the decision to review SAPs in light of their social consequences. In these reviews, social work should position itself to question the wisdom of industrialization and top-down bureaucracy as the principal means of generating work in poor countries. For example, in the heavily populated areas of South Asia (Bangladesh, Bhutan, India, the Maldives, Nepal, Pakistan, and Sri Lanka), unemployed people number between 15 million and 20 million, and underemployment is three to four times as great. The market-driven economy either excludes a substantial sector of the labor force or exploits those who should be legitimately exempt from it, such as children. The social work approach to social policy must be sensitive to the incapacity of mainstream production sectors to absorb all labor resources; the inability of governments to provide entitlements that may help the population acquire employment, education, skills, and market access; and the inability of the social system to reach out to all vulnerable sections of society. Similar considerations are also relevant in other parts of the world. In industrialized countries, as well, there are tendencies for parts of the population to be cut off permanently from the labor market and thus marginalized from society (Acharya & Ramsay, 1995).

Empowering Disadvantaged Groups

The aim of social integration is to create a society for all, in which every individual, each with rights and responsibilities, has an active role to play (UN, 1995). Integration must be based on respect for human rights and freedoms, cultural and religious diversity, the special needs of vulnerable and disadvantaged groups, democratic participation, and the rule of law. If these basic commitments are not adhered to, social integration can mean merely acceptance of and adjustment to prevailing structures and power—that is, submission to the dominant social system. Social integration is a key goal for social work, which should be moving from an emphasis on adjustment of the individual to society to an emphasis on changing society to meet individual needs, including the goals of eradicating poverty and eliminating unemployment.

Today exclusion has many causes, including xenophobia and racism. Large groups of people, such as those with HIV and AIDS, drug abusers, migrant workers, and refugees, are excluded from normal life. Social exclusion can only be counteracted if participation in decision making by such excluded groups is promoted. Social work's traditional role of advocacy for vulnerable groups will have to be supplemented with empowerment strategies. The goal must be to enable excluded groups to be agents of their own social inclusion. Social work in industrialized countries and other parts of the world still have much to learn from the methods advocated by Paulo Freire (1970) and adopted by Latin American social workers, which enabled the profession in that region to emphasize the empowerment of excluded groups.

Empowerment is one of several methods social workers can use in their role as change agents. Davies (1994) discussed a number of these approaches in his book, *The Essential Social Worker.* They emphasize supplying marginalized people with knowledge and tools to ensure their own human and social rights. One method is to work with local, regional, and national power structures to promote, develop, and implement needed policy changes. Another is to identify, involve, and train appropriate and qualified leaders from the community to work in the identification, planning, and implementation of needed programs and services. In addition, the importance of documentation and communication of facts about exclusion and marginalization is emphasized. Social workers' unique knowledge of how people live is of limited use if it is not made available to policymakers, the media, and the general public. Making this knowledge accessible will assist vulnerable groups and may also increase respect for the profession and its expertise (IFSW, 1995).

THE UNITED NATIONS WORLD SUMMIT: IMPLEMENTING THE COMMITMENT

The United Nations World Summit for Social Development increased the importance of social issues on the global agenda. For the first time world leaders agreed to take decisive steps toward eradicating poverty. They also recognized the central role of women when they stated that empowerment of women in society is a key precondition for social development. The Fourth World Conference on Women in Beijing later in 1995 confirmed this statement. The Copenhagen commitment to promote the goal of full employment is also an important step forward, despite the difficulties experienced in fulfilling that goal. Finally, the commitment to promote social integration may serve as the credo of this landmark UN conference:

> We commit ourselves to promoting social integration by fostering societies that are stable, safe and just and that are based on the promotion and protection of human rights, as well as on non-discrimination, tolerance, respect of diversity, equality of opportunity, solidarity, security, and participation of all people, including disadvantaged and vulnerable groups and persons. (UN, 1995, p. 18)

Work toward the implementation of this commitment is an obligation for society as a whole, but is particularly a challenge for social work. Robert

Remo Bissio (1995, p. 4) described his reaction during the preparatory process for the social summit: "A magician traveled from town to town, in days of old, taking a large trunk with him. 'What are you selling?' asked the townspeople. 'Whatever you want,' he said. 'We want peace, justice, health, and warm clothing,' they said. 'I'm sorry,' said the salesman. 'I don't sell fruit, only the seeds.'" Professional social work is a key actor in helping the seeds grow to fruit. The challenge is to be actively involved in implementing this commitment.

IFSW: CREDO, GOALS, AND PROGRAM

What is meant by international social work? Robert L. Barker (1995, p. 194) defines international social work as "a term loosely applied to: (1) international organizations using social work methods or personnel, (2) social work cooperation between countries, and (3) the transfer between countries of methods or knowledge about social work."

International social work is exemplified by IFSW's activities. The organization's historical roots can be traced to 1928, when the International Permanent Secretariat of Social Workers was formed in Paris. The secretariat was active until the outbreak of World War II. After the war, action was taken to create IFSW and the federation was officially founded in 1956. Membership is based on national social worker associations, and today such associations in 59 different countries with more than 430,000 members make up IFSW.

The IFSW Constitution (1996a, pp. 1–2) promulgates the credo of social work and the aims of the organization as follows:

> Social work originates variously from humanitarian, religious and democratic ideals and philosophies; and it has universal application to meet human needs arising from personal–societal interactions, and to develop human potential. Professional social workers are dedicated to service for the welfare and self-fulfillment of human beings: to the development and disciplined use of scientific knowledge regarding human behavior and society; to the development of resources to meet individual, group, national and international needs and aspirations, to the enhancement and improvement of the quality of life of people; and to the achievement of social justice.
>
> Its aims are:
>
> (a) To promote Social Work as a profession through cooperation internationally, especially regarding professional values,

standards, ethics, human rights, recognition, training and working conditions.

(b) To promote the establishment of national associations of social workers.

(c) To support associations in promoting the participation of social workers in social planning and the formulation of social policies, nationally and internationally and the recognition of social work, enhancement of social work training as well as values and standards in social work.

(d) To encourage contacts between social workers of all countries.

(e) To provide means for discussion and the exchange of ideas and experience through meetings, study visits, research projects, exchanges, publications and other methods of communication.

(f) To establish and maintain relations with international organizations relevant to social development and welfare.

(g) To present and promote the point of view of the social work profession to international and national organizations carrying out social planning, social development, social action and welfare programs.

(h) To maintain, promote and amend as necessary the document "Ethics of Social Work—Principles and Standards."

IFSW's major programs reflect the principal international concerns and challenges for social work in the final decade of the 20th century. They include the promotion of human rights, the development of policies on social issues, and the advancement of international ethical standards for social work.

Human Rights and Social Work

The International Association of Schools of Social Work and IFSW have prepared a manual on human rights and social work. The manual, which was published by the United Nations Centre for Human Rights in Geneva in a revised edition in 1994, is based on a belief that greater knowledge and understanding of human rights will improve the actions and interventions of social work professionals. In the introduction to its *International Policy Papers* (1988), IFSW stated

> Social work has, from its conception, been a human rights profession, having as its basic tenet the intrinsic value of every human being and as one of its main aims the promotion of equitable social structures,

> which can offer people security and development while upholding their dignity. (p. 1)

The term "human rights" is used to convey an idea of the totality of rights as identified by the UN. Three distinct types of rights are included. The first, labeled "negative rights," represents civil and political rights as set forth in the *Universal Declaration of Human Rights* (United Nations Centre for Human Rights, 1994). These are rights devised to ensure freedom from any curtailment of individual liberty. The second type encompasses the so-called positive (economic, social, and cultural) rights in the declaration, which are aimed at ensuring social justice, freedom from want, and participation in the social, economic, and cultural aspects of life. The third comprises the "collective" rights: "Everyone is entitled to a social and international order in which the rights and freedoms set forth in this Declaration can be fully realized" (UN Centre for Human Rights, p. 56).

There is a clear connection between the collective rights and the social summit's commitments and thus there is a strong link between a more just and integrated society and the concept of human rights. The social work profession's focus on human needs, and the conviction that these needs are fundamental, require that they are met not as a matter of choice, but as an imperative of basic justice. The full realization of civil and political rights is impossible without enjoyment of economic, social, and cultural rights. Human rights are inseparable from social work theory, values, ethics, and practice. It is therefore difficult to perform social work in a society in which basic human rights are not met. The recognition of the interdependence between human rights and social work practice has led IFSW to focus its work in this area. In addition to the manual for operationalizing human rights concerns in social work practice, IFSW has developed an international policy paper on human rights that proclaims common standards and guidelines in the area of human rights for the work of all professional social workers (IFSW, 1996b).

International Policy on Social Issues

IFSW has also developed a range of other policy papers on social issues, which are often linked to UN instruments, including papers on aging, child welfare, health, HIV/AIDS, migration, peace and disarmament, protection of personal information, refugees, conditions in rural communities, self-help, women, and youths. The policy statements have been developed through a process of deliberation among representatives of social work associations in nations around the globe. An international approach to a major social problem is formulated and an international policy is defined through a democratic process, where all member social work associations are invited to make comments and proposals. Finally, the IFSW General Meeting decides on approval through voting. In this way, social workers from around the world have been able to agree on international platforms for major social work issues. In a diversified world and a profession so often closely linked to local or national environments, it is remarkable that social workers can agree on substantial issues. However, again and again, when social workers meet, consensus can be reached.

The Ethics of Social Work

In 1994 IFSW approved a new document on the ethics of social work. The document is divided in two parts: an international declaration of ethical principles of social work and an international ethical standards for social work. It formulates a set of basic ethical principles for the social work profession that can be adapted to the cultural and social settings in different countries. The document identifies ethical problem areas in the practice of social work and provides guidance on the choice of methods for dealing with ethical issues or problems. Ethical awareness is a necessary part of the professional practice of any social worker, and the commitment to act ethically is an essential aspect of the quality of the services offered to clients. In a more and more complicated world, ethical debate and reflection should be promoted on a continuing basis. This is a major challenge ahead for both international and national organizations of social workers. An IFSW Permanent Committee on Ethical Issues, with members from the five main regions of the world, has been established to expedite this process (IFSW, 1994).

THE FUTURE OF INTERNATIONAL SOCIAL WORK

Where does international social work go from here? The tasks ahead are enormous, but the challenges are also balanced by opportunities. As stated in a recent annual report of the United Nations, "Never before have so many courageous and committed people been involved in world betterment. Never before have nations recognized so clearly that their fate is bound up with each other" (Boutros-Ghali, 1995, p. 362).

The declaration and program of action from the social summit may be the most important documents of the decade. Delegates from 186 countries and the largest gathering yet of world leaders have committed their countries to social progress and development. Nongovernment organizations are also committed to implementing the program of action, as is the UN itself. In response to the core issues of the social summit, the fight against poverty, support for sustainable employment, and the fostering of social integration, international social work has placed itself in the mainstream of social development.

Recognition of the importance of international social issues has increased, and there is a "growing realization that no nation can solve its social problems unilaterally. Experience with the spread of AIDS, drug trafficking and addiction, the disaster at the Chernobyl nuclear power plant, and migration underscore the reality of global interdependence" (Healy, 1995, p. 1509). This awareness will result in the demand for more international knowledge in the area of social development and more demand for social workers who have social development skills. International social work cooperation is needed, both through IFSW and in other arenas, so that professional social workers around the world are able to effectively respond to the challenge.

REFERENCES

Acharya, S., & Ramsay, R. F. (1995). Unemployment in India: Need for grassroots intervention. *IFSW Newsletter, 1,* 7–10.

Barker, R. L. (1995). *The social work dictionary* (3rd ed.) Washington, DC: NASW Press.

Barr, N. (Ed.). (1994). *Labor markets and social policy in Central and Eastern Europe: The transition and beyond.* New York: Oxford University Press.

Bissio, R. R. (Ed.). (1995). *The world: A third world guide 1995/96.* Montevideo, Uruguay: Instituto del Tercer Mundo.

Boutros-Ghali, B. (1995). *Confronting new challenges—Annual report on the work of the organization.* New York: United Nations.

Davies, M. (1994). *The essential social worker* (3rd ed.). Aldershot, England: Arena.

Freire, P. (1970). *Pedagogia de oprimido.* Montevideo, Uruguay: Editorial Tierra Nueva.

Hall, N. (1995). Social work and the eradication of poverty. *IFSW Newsletter, 1,* 3–6.

Healy, L. M. (1995). International social welfare: Organizations and activities. In R. L. Edwards, (Ed.-in-Chief), *Encyclopedia of social work* (19th ed., Vol. 2, pp. 1499–1510). Washington, DC: NASW Press.

Hugman, R. (1996). Professionalization in social work: The challenge of diversity. *International Social Work, 39,* 131–147.

International Federation of Social Workers. (1988). *International policy papers.* Geneva: Author.

International Federation of Social Workers. (1994). *The ethics of social work.* Oslo: Author.

International Federation of Social Workers. (1995). *IFSW Newsletter* (Special edition for the United Nations World Summit for Social Development).

International Federation of Social Workers. (1996a). *Constitution.* Oslo: Author.

International Federation of Social Workers. (1996b). *Policy paper on human rights.* Oslo: Author.

Kramer, D. (1995). *The initial and further training of social workers taking into account their changing role.* Strasbourg, France: Council of Europe.

Richmond, M. E. (1969). *Friendly visiting among the poor.* Montclair, NJ: Patterson Smith. (Original work published 1989)

The Economist pocket world in figures–1996 edition. (1995). London: The Economist Newspaper.

United Nations. (1994). *World social situation in the 1990s.* New York: Author.

United Nations. (1995). *World summit for social development.* New York: Author.

United Nations Centre for Human Rights. (1994). *Human rights and social work.* Geneva: Author.

United Nations Department of Public Information. (1994). *Social integration.* New York: Author.

United Nations Department of Public Information. (1995). *International year for the eradication of poverty.* New York: Author.

11

Social Work Education in an International Context

Current Trends and Future Directions

RALPH GARBER

The end of the 20th century invites millenarian reveries and visions. Expectations for the next century are wishful because issues from the present one are unfinished. Because it is barely more than a century old, social work education is a product of the 20th century. In that time, schools of social work education have increased from just a few at the beginning of the century to more than 1,600 today. It is tempting to project an exponential increase in schools of social work in the 21st century, but their survival may be a more important issue in the future than their rapid, continuing expansion.

The last few years of the 20th century and the first decade of the next could witness a new role for international social work education, or one that departs significantly from the present one. This chapter rests on the other chapters' analyses of social work and the context in which the profession is practiced. Social work education is closely linked to both the past and the future of the profession and to changes in social provision that are expected in the coming decades.

The context in which social work functions and the subcontext for social work education are key determinants in examining the field. Defining the context is more problematic than accepting its relevance. Social work can offer context as the confounding variable without shedding any more light on the question. This chapter narrows the contextual field somewhat in examining social work education. This will include the larger world in which international social work education plays out its roles such as in the United Nations (UN) and the nongovernment organizations in social welfare.

The worldwide contextual reality could focus on the 1995 United Nations World Summit for Social Development and its unfolding consequences, with less attention to services and more to economic and social structuring. In addition, the Socrates Project of the European Community emphasizes function rather than discipline or profession. These developments may change the context in which social work functions and will likely affect the profession and its education (Lorenz, 1994).

The UN itself is under severe strain, and for more than 15 years, the financial and military support expected from the wealthiest nations has not been forthcoming when crises struck. Social welfare needs or substantive rights have not received needed resources even though declarations of rights and social development have been approved by most countries (Boutros-Ghali, 1995). The leaders of the UN at its inception in 1945 and in its first decade accepted the contribution of social work educators and set an expectation for introducing social work education as a necessary adjunct to the delivery of human social services. With world concern for overpopulation, a renewal of UN leadership in the social field in the 1970s permitted international social work education to develop its own resources and those of new schools in developing countries to respond to these concerns (Kendall, 1978; personal communication, Reinhard Wolff, Fachhochschule Berlin, 1993). Because of limited resources it is unlikely that UN initiatives in the social sector will be prominent in the foreseeable future. Social work education will have to look to continental instead of international instruments for its development, as is already evident in Europe, North America, the Chinese-speaking areas of East Asia, southern Africa, and perhaps North Africa and western Asia.

HISTORICAL CONTEXT AND GROWTH

At the turn of the 20th century, the establishment of social work education in the United States preceded international cooperative efforts. There were very few schools in Europe at that time. To make their operations more effective, charities created local social work schools in major cities. There were humble expectations of what social workers, trained or untrained, could do; only Jane Addams and her associates in the social settlement movement believed that no less than world peace and disarmament were suitable goals for social work. These views were shared by some of Addams's European counterparts.

In England, Germany, the United States, and Canada, social agencies created training programs for their staffs with the goal of meeting the agencies' local personnel needs. There were very few government or university program sponsorships at that time. The modern social welfare state, a suitable sponsor, had been instituted in Germany in 1870 and in the United Kingdom just before World War I, but social work training was not included in the legislation. There were fewer than 30 schools or training programs worldwide by 1914. After World War I, there was an upsurge of social welfare development in industrialized countries, which was attributable in part to social legislation in Europe to care for the victims of the war and the unacceptable levels of visible poverty.

The Great Depression of the 1930s found North America and Europe unprepared for the high unemployment and the voluntary sector lacking in social resources to cope with the resulting familial and community dislocations and poverty. The Industrial Revolution of the 19th century had long before shown that countries were unprepared to cope with the damage to individuals, families, and communities caused by industrialization's dislocations, cyclical unemployment, accelerated urbanization, and weakened social institutions. The economic depression of the 1930s produced more of the conditions that had prevailed through the 19th century, but those conditions had become more visible internationally as well as more susceptible to governmental intervention—if governments chose to act (Hobsbawm, 1995).

Although some schools of social work were sharply critical of the social policies of the era (or their absence), the schools did not play important roles in social reform. The German state schools of social work, which had begun under the leadership of Alice Solomon in Berlin in the late 1920s and early 1930s, were decimated or destroyed when the Nazis came to power as a result of the Great Depression and the dislocations after World War I. The accounts of social workers' and social work teachers' defiance of the Nazi regime—or collusion or passive accommodation by some—provide a portrait of social work's role under extreme circumstances.

After World War II there were positive changes, including rebuilding of the economies of the industrialized countries. Decolonization in much of Africa and Asia promised similar success. Promises made during the war to provide freedom from want and oppression were fulfilled with the rapid growth of the welfare state. The new social legislation enacted in many economically advanced countries required personnel with the professional administrative skills to carry out programs. New social work schools were established in these countries as well as in decolonized countries, according to the directives issued by the UN in its early years. Missionaries and district administrators in Africa, China, and India believed that if they could train local people to manage their own services, they would enhance their skills and prepare for their eventual independence from colonial powers. The arrival of independence for the South Asia subcontinent in 1947 and 1948, the revolution in China in 1949, and the decolonization of sub-Saharan Africa that began in the mid-1950s hastened this process with mixed results for social work education. The People's Republic of China closed the several schools of social work that existed in China before 1949. Taiwan, which had no schools of social work, established some in the 1960s, and still more later as its economy grew. South Korea's establishment of social work schools began after the Korean War ended in 1953. Japan, which had a few missionary-established schools before 1941, increased that number during the occupation by U.S. forces from 1945 to 1955, when American-style social welfare structures were created by General Douglas MacArthur.

Africa experienced a number of economic, political, and natural disasters during this period, and social development was stunted in much of the sub-Saharan region. A marginal increase in social provision in East Africa and little in French-speaking West Africa contrast with the development of 20 social work schools or programs in South Africa during the same period. Since 1989 North Africa and the Arab countries have also seen movement toward social work education, despite the ideological opposition of religious fundamentalist groups. This growth is reflected in the recent creation of social work education programs in the North African countries of Egypt, Morocco, Tunisia, and Algeria and the West Asian countries of Kuwait, Saudi Arabia, Jordan, and Lebanon, with Egypt at the geographic center providing the most programs and development. Social work education, which had made a beginning in Eastern Europe before 1939 and immediately after 1945, was transformed and virtually eliminated by the Communist regimes that took over after 1949 in Hungary, Czechoslovakia, and the Baltic states. Poland resisted because of the strong influence of the Catholic church, and some schools continued to function there throughout the period from 1949 to 1989 (Constable & Mehta, 1994).

The world totals grew, and, by the early 1960s, there were about 800 schools of social work. The United States saw a proliferation of undergraduate social work programs in the 1960s and thereafter. Similar growth was experienced during the 1960s in Western Europe, Canada, and Australia. These trends resulted in an increase to more than 1,200 schools by the 1970s. By 1995 there were more than 1,600 schools of social work around the world that were listed in the directory published by the International Association of Schools of Social Work (IASSW) (Dominelli, 1995). The sharp rise in the number of programs in the late 1970s and through the 1980s was partially attributable to industrial developments in Japan and other countries of East Asia, including Korea, Taiwan, Hong Kong, and Singapore. The dismemberment of the Soviet Bloc in 1989 led to the re-establishment of social work and social work education in the countries of Central and Eastern Europe. The shift to elements of market economy in the People's Republic of China also contributed. Social work and social work education were reintroduced and more than 100 new schools were added within five years.

More than 50 schools were established in Russia with financing from the Ministry for Social Protection of Populations and supported through provision of trainers and literature by Dutch, North American, Scandinavian, and British social work educators. The four new schools in the Baltic states received help from a number of countries, including Finland, Denmark, the United States, and Sweden. New schools in Central and Eastern Europe (including the Czech Republic, Slovakia, Hungary, Romania, and Bulgaria) were initiated with support from Germany, Austria, other Western European countries, and the United States. Social work education began in Ukraine and Belarus with support from North American educators and practitioners; in Armenia, the new school was assisted by British schools of social work.

The schools in Central and Eastern Europe were established by their governments and assisted through foreign aid or foreign university initiatives. The external government aid may continue into the next century's first decade, and university researchers will likely retain their interest in these developing areas. The new schools that have been created will also find their own voices and be able to weigh foreign advice more critically. These are positive signs for the near future.

After 1985 the 30 provincial Civil Affairs Administrative Cadre Training Colleges in the People's Republic of China began to incorporate social work–like education, under the guidance of educators from Hong Kong and from the schools in the Asia and Pacific Regional Association for Social Work Education. Ten university-affiliated schools or departments of social work sponsored by the Chinese Ministry of Civil Affairs were added to the central and provincial governments' training programs.

Schools of social work in Latin America, like their countries' governments, have undergone significant changes in the past 20 years. As these countries rid themselves of military dictatorships, governments became, at least nominally, more responsive to their citizenry. Social work educators, despairing of any substantial response from their governments, struck out on their own and adopted popular education and social development theories and practices. They placed great emphasis on social change and reduced the attention to those social work methods concentrated on individual and clinical interventions, which were the preferred approaches of the established and sectarian services.

Social work education is present today in 100 of the 176 UN member countries. There are schools of social work on every continent, and almost all Latin American, North American, and European countries are represented. Social work education is absent in large parts of sub-Saharan Africa, the South Pacific islands, and some of the Asian republics of the former Soviet Union (Dominelli, 1995). Still, it now covers most of the world's population.

INTERNATIONAL ASSOCIATION OF SCHOOLS OF SOCIAL WORK

IASSW is the principal international organization for social work education. With its affiliated regional organizations, it serves about 1,600 educational programs around the world. The association sponsors a biennial international congress and represents social work education at the UN and other international organizations. IASSW also works with the International Federation of Social Workers (IFSW) and the International Council on Social Welfare (ICSW) on cooperative projects, including cosponsorship of the journal *International Social Work* (Hokenstad & Kendall, 1995).

IASSW governance includes an active policy role for the general assembly, which meets in conjunction with the biennial congress. Delegates from member schools; representatives from national, regional, and subregional associations; and representatives from other affiliated groups make up the electoral body. The board of directors, officers, and members at large are elected by the general membership, and each of the associations sends its president or another delegate to the board's annual meetings.

A primary activity of IASSW through the years has been sponsorship of the biennial international congress. Another important function has been representation of the interests and expert knowledge of social work education before international and regional bodies. Cooperative relationships have been established with a number of UN agencies and regional government bodies, including the United Nations Children's Fund; the United Nations Educational, Scientific, and Cultural Organization; the United Nations High Commissioner for Refugees; the World Health Organisation; the

United Nations Development Programme; the Council of Europe; the European Union; the Organization of African Unity; and the Organization of American States (Hokenstad & Kendall, 1995).

International social work education's cooperative efforts began in 1928 and 1929. International social work as an educational effort historically took the form that available resources allowed. The development of parallel or competing associations drawn from the subdisciplines within or alongside social work have eroded some of its centrality as a social education institution. Internationalism as a belief after World War I and again after World War II gave moral support to the IASSW, but it could not compete against nationalist and regionalist pressures that grew from the 1960s and have become more powerful at the end of this century. The centralization in Europe and North America further emphasized the need for other voices and other areas of the world to claim their own importance. Since its beginning IASSW has not achieved a sufficient contributing membership base or sufficient funds to establish an effectively large international office, except for a period during the early 1970s. At that time, UN support for family planning projects allowed the IASSW to expand to a paid staff of five (Kendall, 1978; personal communication, Reinhard Wolff, Fachhochschule Berlin, 1993).

Despite its existence over nearly seven decades, IASSW has had only three paid secretaries-general. Alice Solomon of Germany was IASSW's first chair and president. After World War II, when the organization took up residence in the United States, Katherine A. Kendall of the United States became its first paid staff member in 1971. She stayed until the IASSW moved to Vienna in 1978, when the UN Division of Humanitarian Affairs relocated there. The last two paid executive staff were Marguerite Mathieu of Canada for the first half of the Vienna period (1978 to 1985), and Vera Mehta of India for the last period in Vienna from 1985 to 1993 when the UN Division of Humanitarian Affairs returned to New York after the Austrian government could no longer provide financial support. Since 1993 IASSW has re-established the volunteer organizational structure it had until 1971. Its office is now at the home of the incumbent volunteer president—in Canada from 1993 to 1996 and in the United Kingdom from 1996 until 2000.

Because of the national association and regional and subregional associational structure of IASSW, social work schools can choose to affiliate only with their national and regional associations and not become paying members of the international group. Fewer than a quarter of all programs and about 2 percent of all social work educators are now paying members of IASSW. No sanctions or accrediting restrictions are imposed, or could be imposed, to encourage membership. However, legitimizing social work education by an external international authority is a useful, positive incentive for membership. Eastern European countries and some in Asia have used IASSW membership for this purpose.

DISCIPLINARY INTEGRITY FOR INTERNATIONAL SOCIAL WORK EDUCATION

As one of a discipline's functions, the development of knowledge can be used as a test of its integrity, both nationally and internationally. The range of skill- or method-focused education within social work is not fully mapped. There are many subdisciplines, such as work with groups, clinical therapeutic social work, social administration, and social development. Each subdiscipline has developed its own literature and conducts conferences and seminars and publishes its own journals. There are attempts to control the role of the social work curriculum and describe the discipline of social work in terms of subdisciplines. Schools of social work also divide their curricular offerings along other subdisciplinary lines. Fields of practice lead to the organization of courses along such specific dimensions of services as child welfare, family services, mental health, probation and corrections, or rehabilitation. A social problem approach helps organize the curriculum to cover all the aspects of specific problems, such as poverty, racism, sexism, and ageism.

Although these subdisciplines create fragmentation, they are not as problematic as the division between basic and applied disciplines in social work education. Educators who identify with the basic discipline rely on the social sciences or humanities and see themselves primarily as adherents of their discipline, such as economist, psychologist, and so forth, and only secondarily as involved in social work. Those who identify with applied discipline more often consider social work as their professional home. These divisions represent social work as a discipline in multiple array, acting in federated arrangements.

These challenges to disciplinary integrity have been particularly problematic during the social transition of the 20th century. Countries in Eastern Europe had no social work education for 40 or more years and recruited from psychology, pedagogy, law and criminology, and new programs in sociology to begin new social work education programs. Academics in philosophy and the social sciences in former Communist countries and the People's Republic of China provided leadership in conceptualizing this discipline. Their readings of Western literature were transformed, sometimes within a socialist ideology, to create an operational response to social need at the levels of individual, family, and community. These academics had mixed motivations, including the adventure of examining a new way of organizing thought and exploring social phenomena, and the opportunity to get in on the ground floor in a discipline with the potential of gaining acceptance from authorities. This dilemma was particularly apparent in Russia, which had no tradition of social work, or any practical or theoretical exposure to the profession or its academic counterpart. In 1992 the Russian Ministry of Social Protection stated that all universities were to serve as branches of Moscow State University, and a single text compendium culled from Western social work education was required for all branches. Although the operating principle of social development, which encourages and facilitates indigenous forms of social organization and mutual help, was emphasized in this effort, it did not result in an integrated body of knowledge.

On the other hand, there has been a considerable amount of pairing of schools across the world with resultant faculty, student, and materials exchanges (Erasmus Projects, National Reports, 1996). It is still too early to assess the impact of these cooperative efforts on disciplinary thinking. The example of the Hong Kong Schools of Social Work is instructive. Educators from Hong Kong became supporters of social work education in China shortly after Deng Xiao Ping's economic reforms were instituted in the late 1970s. The Hong Kong schools and their faculties acted out of ideological motivation: helping China enter the 21st century with its newly tolerated market economy. That economic change was causing social and personal disruption, including massive dislocation of populations. The cooperation anticipated the return of Hong Kong to China in 1997 so that Hong Kong's leadership for the mainland in the social as well as the economic arena was established. It provided both curriculum development consultation and research opportunities and certainly has made an important contribution to the development of social work education in China. However, the resulting programs of social work education set up by the Chinese Ministry of Civil Affairs still remain to be assessed for disciplinary integrity.

Many schools of social work in Europe, Latin America, and North America have other disciplines represented on their teaching staff. These include psychology and psychiatry for the interpersonal theories; sociology, anthropology, and social psychology for the group and sociocultural problem theories; political science, economics, and law for the social policy theories; and, in some schools, philosophy and religious thought for the humanistic and ethical theories. This attests to the eclecticism of social work and its dynamic molding of a derived or applied theory out of other disciplines. Still, the lack of disciplinary integrity creates problems within individual countries and even greater barriers to global consistency in social work education.

INTERNATIONAL STANDARD SETTING FOR SOCIAL WORK EDUCATION

Accreditation of academic standards in schools of social work by national accrediting bodies is available in only a few countries. There also are national civil service accreditations or certifications in many nations, which attest to social work's establishment as a continuing function in those countries. This form of accreditation limits the global generalization of social work education. Ministries of social affairs, social protection, civil affairs, and social welfare in different countries demand commitments from their training institutions, which often do not have the independence of colleges and universities. These ministries do not have the highest status in their respective countries' governments and do not convey prestige to social work.

To discuss even minimal international standards in social work education, much additional—and more accurate—data are needed. There are no worldwide data on the number and qualifications of teachers of social work, the number and characteristics of social work students, variations in curricula, and type of practicum. Data on the length and level of training in different countries are available, but in some cases are dated. Most available information simply provides a description of programs, with no basis for comparisons to answer even the most basic questions.

There are, however, several individual country reports, and a European survey of 21 countries has been published (Brauns & Kramer, 1988), but it made no claims for accuracy or statistical content. A subsequent survey by the same authors, with a different intent and focus, was completed in the summer of 1996 but has not been made available for distribution at the time of this writing. The UN has no survey data pertinent to social work education, but its 1987 conference on social welfare alludes to significant efforts by UN member states to enlarge on and improve training for social welfare.

Thus international standards setting for social work education—or even a debate about its usefulness—must await more accurate and comprehensive information about programs, educators, and students around the world. Data are urgently needed and should be a priority for international organizations.

SOCIAL WORK EDUCATION AT THE TURN OF THE CENTURY: AN ASSESSMENT

The development of social services and social welfare provisions have provided the context for social work education in the 20th century. Although the growth of the field has been exponential, the problems of identify, standards, and disciplinary integrity remain.

An assessment of social work education's prospects as it enters the next century does not produce a rosy picture. The too-high level of expectation may partly explain why the future does not look bright. If we are so rich in numbers and diversity, why have we not gone further in the development of a discipline? The relative absence of basic and comparative data limits any valid assessment of worldwide trends and confines conclusions to informed observations, but the potential exists for overcoming this limitation. Established forms of international organization provide the vehicles through which such data gathering can occur, and the technology of information processing may facilitate that process even before the next century arrives.

The transformation of the welfare state, since the 1970s in Europe and North America and since the 1980s everywhere, may auger different outcomes for social work education's development in the next century. Countries' diminishing commitments to their social welfare provisions and to international aid for less developed countries has been notable during the last two decades of the 20th century. Passing the responsibility to lower administrative and political jurisdictional levels will result in a status quo reminiscent of the period before World War II, with its attendant diminution of need for social workers. The much needed self-help, mutual help, and public education for the basics of health and physical health have had an unanticipated consequence of removing some of the interpretive functions usually performed by social workers. Recent actions of national legislatures include delisting, declassifying, and removing eligibility of social work clients. Now some countries are eliminating entitlements long fought for, and for which social work had staked its claim as advocate and provider.

All is not lost, however. The industrialization of East Asia and other sectors of the world along with the re-emergence of social work in the former Soviet Bloc countries may lead to a reinvention of social work. The postindustrial or "information society" may require new forms of interpersonal and social interventions that have only begun to be explored.

As the century turns, these and other global developments provide challenge and opportunity to social work education around the world.

First steps toward meeting this challenge will be obtaining more accurate data about the current state of social work education and more clearly defining the global state of the art. At its Hong Kong meeting in 1996, IASSW set up a task force to carry out a worldwide census on social work education. It also asked IFSW to join in setting forth a definitive working definition of social work as an international discipline. Also, IASSW, ICSW, IFSW, and the social pedagogues in Europe have combined their efforts to arrive at definitions and descriptions of some social work functions (Erasmus Projects, National Reports, 1996). They have issued a preliminary report and expect a final report by 1998.

During the next decade, there will be considerable pressure on the social professions and disciplines to reconcile their differences. These pressures are coming from provincial, state, and national governments as well as from regional bodies. The three international bodies of IASSW, ICSW, and IFSW and other groups will convene in Jerusalem in 1998 to further formalize their relationship and consider a joint planning function for the beginning of the next century.

Social work education's response to these challenges over the next five years will hold as much promise as risk. The scope of social work education, with its self-proclaimed "inclusive" definition, will be tested, but expansion to encompass much of social development and accommodate social pedagogy and social policy, planning, and administration is possible. The social activist and popular education movements should have no ideological conflict with social work education or practice. The prospects for such international cooperation, active collaboration, and joint educational efforts are brighter now than they have been in the past, although the problems of identity and hegemony will remain. It may be that more pronounced divisions are more likely than any resolution. Only the prospect of mutual benefit may motivate better cooperation.

REFERENCES

Boutros-Ghali, B. (1995). *Confronting new challenges: Annual report on the work of the organization.* New York: United Nations.

Brauns, H. J., & Kramer, D. (1988). *Social work education in Europe: A comprehensive description of social work education in 21 European countries.* Frankfurt, Germany: Deutsche Verein für Öffentliche und Privat Fürsorge.

Constable, R., & Mehta, V. (1994). *Changing horizons in education for social work and human services in Eastern Europe*. Chicago: Lyceum.

Dominelli, L. (Ed.). (1995). *The International Association of Schools of Social Work Directory 1995*. Sheffield, England: University of Sheffield.

Erasmus Projects, National Reports. (1996, July). *France, Germany, Great Britain, Italy, Netherlands, Portugal, Spain, Sweden*. Coblenz, Germany: Erasmus Evaluation Conference.

Hobsbawm, E. (1995). *Age of extremes: The short twentieth century, 1914–1991*. London: Abacus.

Hokenstad, M. C., & Kendall, K. A. (1995). International social work education. In R. L. Edwards (Ed.-in-Chief), *Encyclopedia of social work* (19th ed., Vol. 2, pp. 1511–1520). Washington, DC: NASW Press.

Kendall, K. A. (1978). *Reflections on social work education 1950–1978*. New York and Vienna: International Association of Schools of Social Work.

Lorenz, W. (1994). *Social work in a changing Europe*. London and New York: Routledge.

Index

Q

R

S

T

U

About the Editors

M. C. Hokenstad, PhD, is the Ralph S. and Dorothy P. Schmitt Professor in the Mandel School of Applied Social Sciences and professor of International Health in the School of Medicine at Case Western Reserve University. He has long been active in international organizations and currently serves as membership secretary of the International Association of Schools of Social Work and as a member of the United Nations Non-Governmental Committee on Aging. Dr. Hokenstad has been editor-in-chief of the *International Social Work Journal* and has published extensively in the fields of international social welfare, social gerontology, and social work education. His books include *Participation in Teaching and Learning: An Idea Book for Social Work Educators* (with Barry Rubgy, 1977), *Linking Health Care and Social Services* (with Roger Rituo, 1982), *Gerontological Social Work: International Perspectives* (with Katherine Kendall, 1988), and *Profiles in International Social Work* (with James Midgley and S. K. Khinduka, 1992). He has received two Fulbright Awards for teaching and research in Scandinavia and has been a visiting professor and program consultant at several universities in Europe and Asia.

James Midgley, PhD, is the Harry and Riva Specht Professor of Public Social Services and dean of the School of Social Welfare at the University of California at Berkeley. He has published widely on international social work, social development, and social policy. His major books include *Professional Imperialism: Social Work in the Third World* (1961); *Social Security, Inequality, and the Third World* (1984), *Comparative Social Policy and the Third World* (with Stewart MacPherson, 1987), *Profiles in International Social Work* (with M. C. Hokenstad and S. K. Khinduka, 1992), *Social Development: The Development Perspective in Social Welfare* (1995), and *Social Welfare in Global Context* (1997). He has also contributed to many leading social policy, social work, and development journal studies.

About the Contributors

Lena Dominelli, PhD, is a professor at the University of Southampton in England. She has conducted research and published extensively in the fields of social work and social policy. Her principal published books include *Love and Wages* (1988), *Feminist Social Work* (with E. McLeod, 1989), *Women and Community Work* (1990), *Women across Continents: Feminist Comparative Social Policy* (1991), *Anti-Racist Probation Practice* (with others, 1995), and *Sociology for Social Work* (1997).

Ralph Garber, DSW, is professor emeritus at the University of Toronto and past president of the International Association of Schools of Social Work. He has been a social work teacher, lecturer, and consultant in China, Japan, India, Sri Lanka, Israel, Eastern and Central Europe, and Southern Africa and has served as dean of three schools of social work in the United States and Canada.

Janet George, PhD, is senior lecturer and head of the Department of Social Work, Social Policy, and Sociology at the University of Sydney. Her research focus is on health policy, with particular interests in aging, gender, ethnicity and service delivery, social development, and social work education in the Asian Pacific region.

Marie D. Hoff, PhD, is associate professor of social welfare policy and community organization practice at the School of Social Work, Boise State University. With John G. McNutt she is co-editor of *The Global Environmental Crisis: Implications for Social Welfare and Social Work* (1994). She has published evaluations of social programs, community organization models, and social action research and a variety of studies on the effects of environmental concerns in human welfare and social justice.

Tom Johannesen, DiplSW, is secretary general and chief executive officer of the International Federation of Social Workers. After a 10-year career as a social worker and administrator, he served as executive director of the Norwegian Association of Social Workers for 10 years. Mr. Johannesen is a member of several advisory and coordination committees for international social work conferences and is active in international projects.

Ronald J. Mancoske, DSW, is a professor of social work at Southern University in New Orleans. He chairs the concentration in Health/Mental Health. His research and community activities are focused on HIV/AIDS services.

Vera Mehta, PhD, is special assistant to the Special Representative of the Secretary General of the United Nations for the former Yugoslav Republic of Macedonia.

Rodreck Mupedziswa, MSc, is deputy head at the School of Social Work, Affiliate College, University of Zimbabwe. His publications include the highly acclaimed book *Uprooted: Refugees and Social Work in Africa* (1993).

Antonin Wagner, PhD, is dean of the Zurich School of Social Work and professor of economics at the University of Zurich. He serves on the editorial board of the *Scandinavian Journal of Social Welfare*. In 1996 he was elected president of the International Society for Third-Sector Research. From 1984 to 1991, he chaired the European Regional Group of the International Association of Schools of Social Work.

Issues in International Social Work
Global Challenges for a New Century

Cover design by Ingrid Gehle, Gehle Design

Interior book design and composition by Christine Cotting,
UpperCase Publication Services, using
Stone Serif and Stone Sans

Printed by Graphic Communications, Inc., on 60# Windsor

(Order form on reverse side)

ORDER FORM

	Title	Item #	Price	Total
__	Issues in International Social Work	2804	$26.95	________
__	Successful Community Leadership	2855	$25.95	________
__	Community Building	2928	$29.95	________
__	Organizing	1972	$32.95	________
__	How People Get Power	2367	$20.95	________
			Subtotal	________
		+ 10% postage and handling		________
			Total	________

❒ I've enclosed my check or money order for $ ____________.

❒ Please charge my ❒ NASW Visa* ❒ Other Visa ❒ MasterCard

Credit Card Number ____________________ Expiration Date ____________

Signature ______________________________

**Use of this card generates funds in support of the social work profession.*

Name ______________________________

Address ______________________________

City ______________ State/Province ______________

Country ______________ Zip ______________

Phone ______________ E-mail ______________

NASW Member # (if applicable) ______________________________

(Please make checks payable to NASW Press. Prices are subject to change.)

NASW PRESS

P. O. Box 431
Annapolis JCT, MD 20701
USA

Credit card orders call
1-800-227-3590
(In the Metro Wash., DC, area, call 301-317-8688)
Or fax your order to 301-206-7989
Or order online at http://www.naswpress.org

Visit our Web site at http://www.naswpress.org.

IISWBI98